Mason Jar Crafts

DIY Projects for Adorable and Rustic Decor, Clever Storage, Inventive Lighting and Much, Much More

Lauren Elise Donaldson

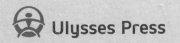

Ulysses Press

Published in the U.S. by
Ulysses Press
P.O. Box 3440
Berkeley, CA 94703
www.ulyssespress.com

ISBN: 978-1-61243-185-7
Library of Congress Control Number 2013931797

Printed in the United States by Bang Printing

10 9 8 7 6 5 4 3 2 1

Acquisitions Editor: Kelly Reed
Managing Editor: Claire Chun
Editor: Lauren Harrison
Proofreader: Elyce Berrigan-Dunlop
Design and layout: Michelle Thompson | Fold & Gather Design

Distributed by Publishers Group West

Contents

Introduction

As a kid, I eagerly observed as my grandma and aunt preserved their homegrown vegetables and fruit in canning jars. They packed them away in their cupboards only to have them reappear at the most opportune times, transformed as marinara sauce on pasta or berry jam on scones. For me, the jars stood for little more than delicious meals made with love. Years later when I started blogging in 2010, I was introduced to these jars again. Now far removed from the kitchen, the same Mason jars from my youth were presented in an entirely different light. The jars may have looked the same but they were new, exciting, something I had never seen before.

In fact, Mason jars have changed relatively little since the 1850s when they were invented. The classic shape and iconic lettering is truly timeless. Even the new jars have that vintage charm, and yet the simplicity feels modern. The dualism of old and new may seem like a happy accident but, like all good design, this deliberate union is what makes the Mason jar great. I believe this is the reason for its surge in popularity over the last few years. Anyone with an appreciation for design and a creative mind will see the Mason jar for what it really is: a blank canvas.

With the widespread use of blogs, photo-sharing social media, and websites like Pinterest, creative ideas can spread like wildfire. As a blogger, I first began noticing Mason jars used at weddings and other events. Without the preserves, the jars were free to act as drink glasses, candle holders, and candy dishes. But that was just the beginning. As I explored further, I found jars transformed into coffee mugs, chandeliers, soap dispensers, flower pots, lamps, and organizers, to name a few. I began experimenting with them on my own, and Mason jars quickly became a staple in my craft toolkit. I continue to use them constantly and find I never regret having a variety of sizes on hand.

The projects in *Mason Jar Crafts* were written with the dreamer in mind, someone who does not just see a canning jar but an opportunity. Explore this book and allow these unique projects to ignite a passion for these jars. The craft techniques found within will not only encourage you to make these specific projects but also serve as catalysts for future artistic endeavors. Originally I understood canning jars little beyond the realm of my grandma's kitchen. They stood for family, nourishment, and love. To me, they still represent those ideals. But the definition is an extensive one. Instead of being defined in a single manner, I believe Mason jars symbolize uninhibited creativity. What will these jars mean to you?

Enjoy!

~Lauren Elise Donaldson

❚ Ball and Kerr Mason jars are still manufactured today. New jars are readily available for purchase. Along with a plethora of online vendors, many other retailers carry Mason jars; look in local grocery stores, craft stores, home improvement stores, and warehouse food supply stores. New Mason jars are significantly cheaper than vintage ones; they often can cost less than $1 each.

❚ Although manufactured by the same company, Ball and Kerr jars vary slightly in their logos and details. Ball jars often have fruit printed into the glass; they also list measurements along the side, similar to a measuring cup. Kerr jars are simpler with just the Kerr label. For certain projects, it is easier to work with Kerr jars. Use them if you need a smooth, flat surface.

❚ Mason jars come in regular and wide-mouth varieties. Wide-mouth jars have a straight silhouette while regular-mouth jars taper in at the top. The opening in regular-mouth jars is approximately 2½ inches in diameter and in wide-mouth jars, approximately 3 inches in diameter. Quart, pint, and half-pint are the most common sizes. A quart jar is 32 ounces, a pint is 16, and a half-pint is 8. All three have the option of regular or wide-mouth.

❚ Wash Mason jars with water or wipe clean with rubbing alcohol before painting. This ensures that grease and other impurities are removed.

❚ Baking Mason jars in the oven could potentially result in cracked glass. Be aware of this and proceed with caution. Always bake jars on a tray to catch glass in case it breaks. Drastic temperature changes will increase the possibility of cracks. To avoid this, put jars in a cold oven and slowly bring it up to temperature. When you are finished, allow jars to cool down in the oven before removing them.

❚ When drilling into the jars, be aware that this can cause cracks. The drill bit gets hot and exposes the glass to extreme temperatures. In some cases, the entire jar can shatter. In case this happens, you need to be protected, so always work with gloves, safety goggles, and a dust mask. Follow the steps outlined on page 124 and proceed slowly. Steady drilling and water will keep the temperature down and preserve the glass

Basic Tools

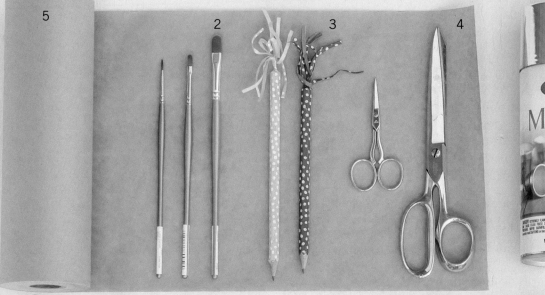

1. Various Mason jars
2. Paint brushes
3. Pencils
4. Scissors
5. Butcher paper
6. Spray paint
7. Various glues
8. Wire
9. Metal lids & bands
10. Wire cutters
11. Metal ruler
12. X-Acto knife
13. Glue gun sticks
14. Hot glue gun
15. Drill
16. Cutting mat

6

16

15

7

14

13

11

12

Common Jar Sizes

Half-pint
8 oz

Regular-mouth pint
16 oz

Quart
32 oz

Wide-mouth pint
16 oz

Quilted jelly
12 oz

Wide-mouth pint
16 oz

Half-pint
8 oz

Mason Jar Terminology

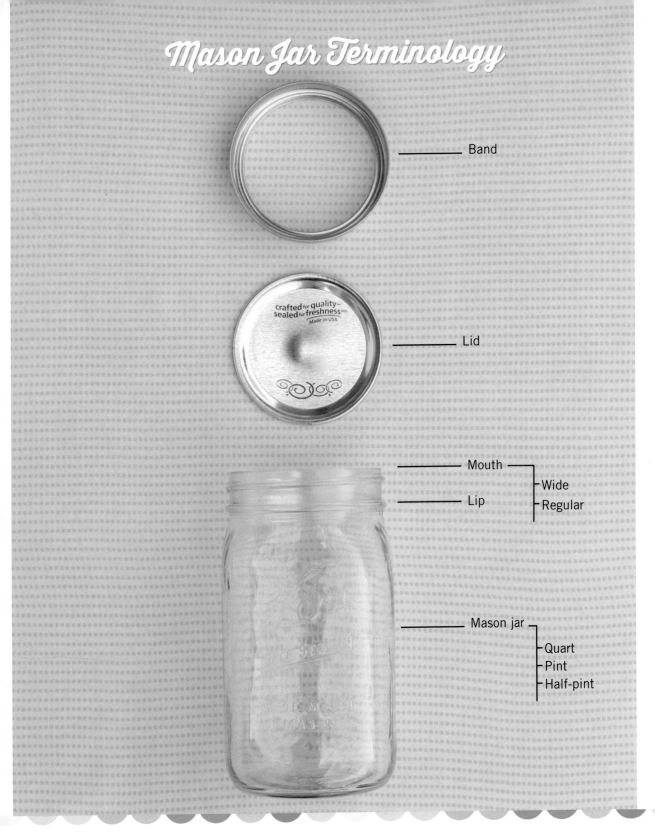

Band

Lid

crafted for quality~
sealed for freshness
Made in USA

Mouth ⎤ Wide
Lip ⎦ Regular

Mason jar ⎤ Quart
          ⎥ Pint
          ⎦ Half-pint

Home Decor

Colorblocked Air Plant Terrariums

Difficulty Rating ▮▮

Air plants are great alternatives for those who enjoy greenery but not the upkeep. After all, not everyone is born with a green thumb. Worry-free plants deserve to be displayed with some glitz and glamour, and these gilded terrariums are one stylish solution. An easy project as well, this DIY only requires a few components, some of which may be found in your own cupboard. Air plants do not require soil to grow so they can be perched on top of any surface or material. Not only is this easy maintenance, but it also allows for total freedom when it comes to display.

Materials

Quart- and/ or pint-size Mason jars	Painter's tape	Dried navy or pinto beans
	Spray paint	Air plants
Butcher paper		

1. Prep your Mason jar by making sure it is clean and that the surface is ready to take paint.

2. Thoroughly cover your work area with butcher paper. Spray paint has a tendency to get everywhere so cover anything valuable that may be in its path.

3 Position painter's tape on your Mason jar in the configuration of your choice.

Press the tape down firmly to prevent paint from seeping underneath. Thoroughly cover the portion of the jar that will not be painted.

4 Put your Mason jar upside down on the butcher paper and spray-paint the jar. Do a thorough coat, covering all the exposed glass.

5 Start to pull the tape up right away, before the paint can fully dry. This will minimize tearing when the tape is removed.

6 Allow the paint to dry overnight.

7 Fill the Mason jar with navy or pinto beans.

8 Display the air plant on top of the beans.

Extra Tips

Plant Care Tip: Keep a spray bottle on hand to easily water the air plants. Air plants need very little attention. An occasional spray or a soak in water, once a week or even once every two weeks should keep them plenty content. Follow specific plant care instructions.

This example uses dried navy or pinto beans. Give other dried foodstuffs a try like rice, black beans, or lentils. Coffee beans are an aromatic alternative as well.

Woodland Herb Garden

Difficulty Rating ▮ ▯ ▯

nyone who spends time in the kitchen under-stands the benefit of fresh herbs and spices. No matter the size of your home, a small kitchen garden can be tended to yield savory flavors. If your collection of herbs is clogging up valuable counter or windowsill space, start a vertical garden instead. These wooden plaques may be practical but they are also a beautiful focal point in any kitchen.

Materials

Inkjet printer	Screwdriver	Wire cutters
Paper	1-hole D-ring hangers	Needle-nose pliers
Tracing paper	½-inch screws	Potted herbs
Pencil	1½-inch gold cup hooks	*Font Used: Jacques & Gilles by Emily Lime*
Oval country wood plaques		
Thin paint brush	Half-pint-size Mason jars	
Metallic bronze acrylic paint	14-gauge gold wire	

1. Using computer software, layout the names of each of your herbs. In this example, basil, oregano, rosemary, and thyme were used. Print out these labels. Copy each label on tracing paper in pencil.

2. On the back of the tracing paper, write over the underside of the labels. When finished, turn the tracing paper back over to the front.

3. Position each label over the wood plaques, centered at the top. Firmly trace back over the labels, imprinting the letters into the wood. Remove the tracing paper.

4. Using a thin brush, paint over the labels with bronze acrylic. Allow the paint to dry before proceeding.

5 Attach one D-ring hanger to the back of each wood plaque with ½-inch screws. One hanger is sufficient to carry the weight of one jar.

6 Five inches down from the top of the wood plaque, mark a center point. Twist in a cup hook at this point. Repeat this with the other plaques.

7 Remove the metal lids and bands from the Mason jars.

8 Cut one 14-inch piece of wire per jar. Wrap the wire around the lip of the jar. Cross the wires where the 2 ends meet.

9 Clamp on to the wire ends with the pliers and twist them together twice.

10 With one end of the remaining wire, form a loop. Wrap the other end around the loop and cut any excess wire. Add wire hangers to each jar.

11 Plant herbs in each of the jars. Hang the jars from their respective wood plaques.

Extra Tips

These plaques were designed to form an indoor kitchen garden, but sometimes plants need time outdoors. Because the jars can be removed from the wood plaques, they can be transported outside whenever necessary. Set up the cup hooks on a wall or fence in a sunny spot in your yard as an alternative.

As the plants continue to thrive and grow, they will need larger containers. Consider repotting the herbs in bigger Mason jars or in pots outside.

"Hello" Welcome Lamp

Difficulty Rating ❚ ❚ ❚ ❚ ❚

Say hello to all your guests with this welcoming lamp. Placed in an entryway, living room, or guest bedroom, it will offer a friendly greeting upon entering any space. The chambray and white color palette feels fresh and modern, and the polka dots add a touch of whimsy. Switch out fabric or paint colors to better complement your home's style. This project has many components and steps, and it requires the use of hardware and power tools. It takes some patience, but once all the materials are gathered, the process should run smoothly.

Materials

Scanner	Vintage chambray fabric	Two ½-inch screws
"Hello" template (see Template Workbook, page 121)	Staple gun	Single snap-in socket cord set with switch
Inkjet printer	Freezer paper	
8.5 x 11-inch paper	Cutting mat	Light bulb
	X-Acto knife	Screwdriver
Scotch tape	Iron	*Font Used: Channel by Måns Grebäck*
18 x 18-inch piece of ½-inch MDF board	White fabric paint	
Pencil	Sponge brush	
1-inch spade bit or drill bit	12-ounce quilted jelly Mason jar with metal band	
Drill	Large nail	
Scissors	Hammer	

1. Scan the "Hello" template from the Workbook and size it to 18 inches square. Print it out and assemble it on three sheets of 8.5 x 11-inch paper. Tape those pages together. Position the template over the MDF board and line up the edges. Mark the location of the center of the "o" onto the board. Remove the template.

2. Using a 1-inch spade bit, drill a hole through the MDF at the center location marked in Step 1.

3. Cut down the chambray fabric to 21 x 21 inches so that there is an excess of 1½ inches around the edges of the MDF board. Center the fabric over the MDF. Fold back the 1½-inch border along one side and use the staple gun to staple the fabric to the MDF. Fold each of the other 3 sides back and staple them. You can also replace the staple gun with a hot glue gun.

4. Cut a small hole in the fabric directly above the hole in the MDF. The light bulb will pass through this hole later on.

5. Cut out an 18 x 18-inch piece of freezer paper. Place the template over the freezer paper and set both on top of a cutting mat. Make sure the glossy side of the freezer paper is facing down. Use an X-Acto knife to cut out the word "hello" from the template. Then cut out the polka dots. Discard the paper template.

6 Place the new freezer paper template on top of the chambray, glossy side facing down in contact with the fabric. On a high heat setting, iron the freezer paper to the fabric. The heat seals the two together.

7 Dab white fabric paint over the exposed chambray. A dabbing motion will provide more even coverage and minimize excess paint from running. Once the word "hello" and the polka dots are painted, carefully pull up the edge of the freezer paper and remove the entire template. Allow the paint to dry before proceeding.

8 Take the Mason jar band and lay it flat on the cutting mat. With a nail and hammer, punch out two holes on either side of the band.

9 Position the band over the drilled hole. Hold the band in place and drill in the screws through the holes punched in Step 8. This should strongly secure the band to the MDF.

10 Take the light socket and insert it in from the back of the MDF board. Fit it into place.

11 Screw in the light bulb from the front. Place the Mason jar over the bulb and screw it into the band. Plug in and illuminate your new light.

Extra Tips

To minimize time with an X-Acto knife, use a digital craft cutter (i.e., the Silhouette Cameo) to cut out the template for this project. These craft printers can cut any intricate shape or design, saving you time and providing a much cleaner cut. They usually include computer software that streamlines the process of cutting your own designs. These machines are helpful for many craft projects and are also popular with scrapbookers.

Choose fabric that complements your decor and personal color palette. For a feminine space, use a floral print. Cover the plywood in burlap for a rustic touch or linen for a French countryside look. Remove the polka dots. Paint stripes instead. Use a bold color or an animal print for a child's space. This lamp has a lot of versatility.

Swap out "hello" for other words that contain the letter "o" like "good night," "love," or "joy," or personalize the lamp with family names.

Modern Macramé Hanging

Difficulty Rating ▮ ▮ ▮

Rethink the art of macramé and update its look to something colorful and modern. All that you need to make your own plant hangers is twisted mason line. This inexpensive material can be found at home improvement stores, it knots easily, and is soft to the touch. It's readily available in white and neon hues, but it's possible to find a few other colors online too. The knotting and braiding techniques used in this tutorial are basic. Add more strands of mason line to create more intricate patterns.

Materials

Twisted mason line in various colors

Scissors

Quart- and pint-size Mason jars

Butcher paper

Spray paint

Succulent or hanging plant

1 Cut 16 strands of mason line to 4 feet each. In this example there are three colors being used—white, orange, and yellow—and 4 strands should be orange, 4 strands should be yellow, and 8 strands should be white. On one end, leave about 7 inches and then tie a knot.

2 Split up the line into 4 groups of 4 strands. Two of the groups will consist of orange and white line and the other two groups will consist of yellow and white line.

3 Take one of the groups and tie a knot about 2 inches from the previous large knot. Do the same thing to the remaining three groups.

4 Take one of the orange groups and one of the yellow groups. From the orange group, take one orange strand and one white strand and separate it out. From the yellow group, take one yellow strand and one white strand and separate it out. Bring those 4 strands together and tie a knot 2 inches away from the previous knot.

5 Do the same thing with the other groups, bringing together and then knotting the orange and yellow strands.

6 For the next set of knots, you want to return the orange and yellow strands back to their original groups. The groups will look like they did in Step 2, with oranges and yellows separated out. Again tie a knot 2 inches away from the previous knot for all 4 groups.

7 Continue this pattern a couple more times.

8 When you are finished, slip the jar between the knotted mason line. It will act as a holder to catch and carry the weight of the jar. Make sure you have enough knots and add more if necessary. Remove the jar and set it aside for now.

9 Now you will braid the remaining length of line in each of the groups. There are 4 strands per group, so you will not use the normal 3-strand technique. Take one group at a time and space out the strands. Put the 2 colored strands on the outside and the 2 white strands on the inside. For this example, the strands will be labeled A, B, C, and D from left to right.

10 Take strand B and move it all the way to the right over strands C and D.

11 Take strand C and move it all the way to the left under strand A. Now the strand configuration will be C - A - D - B.

12 Take strand D and move it all the way to the left over strands C and A.

13 Take strand A and move it all the way to the right under strand B. The configuration is now D - C - B - A.

14 Take strand C and move it to the right over strands B and A.

15 Take strand B and move it to the left under strand D. The configuration is now B - D - A - C.

16 Take strand A and move it to the left over strands B and D.

17 Take strand D and move it to the right under strand C. The configuration is now back to the original A - B - C - D.

18 Following this pattern, braid each of the 4 groups. Tie a knot when you reach the end.

19 Tie one large knot to join all 4 groups together. You can hang the planter from this large knot.

20 Set the Mason jar on butcher paper and give it a coat of spray paint. Allow it to thoroughly dry.

21 Plant your succulent in the Mason jar following any guidelines for your specific variety.

22 Carefully position the jar in the macramé planter and hang.

Extra Tips

The twisted mason line comes in a limited color palette and not everyone is agreeable to neon. Leave out the color and just use the white line. Or if you still want color, try dyeing the line with fabric dye. You can soak the mason line and dye it to match any color palette.

Different kinds of yarn, cord, ribbon, and twine are other possible materials for this DIY. Make sure the material is strong enough to hold the weight of your plant and jar.

Mason Clock

Difficulty Rating ▮ ▮ ▮ ▮ ▮

Mason jars may have been developed for use in food canning, but now they can actually help you keep time. With a few minor adjustments you can make your own Mason jar clock and put this timeless design out on display. For this example, the jars were painted sky blue and cherry red with contrasting white hands for a fresh, modern look. Choose your favorite colors or even experiment by painting with patterns. Remember this project involves drilling a hole in the glass. Take the time to follow the safety instructions laid out in this tutorial. This endeavor can be dangerous, but if you take the right precautions and equip yourself with the correct tools, this project is feasible and fairly simple.

Materials

Pint-size Mason jar	Dust mask/ particulate respirator	15⁄16-inch stem clock mechanism kit
Drill	Watering can or hose	Super glue
3/8-inch diamond drill bit	Marker	
Towel	Sandpaper	
Gloves	Butcher paper	
Safety goggles	Spray paint in various colors	

1 Remove the metal band and lid from the Mason jar.

2 You will want to complete this project outside or in a garage since you will be handling glass. Set up your workspace ahead of time and make sure you are prepared before proceeding. You will need your Mason jar, a drill, a ⅜-inch diamond drill bit, a towel, gloves to protect your hands, safety goggles for eye protection, and a particulate respirator to fully cover your nose and mouth. Also set up a water source. In this example, a watering can was used so that water could be repeatedly applied to the point of contact between the drill and the glass. A light stream of water from a hose would be effective as well. The water is necessary to keep the drill bit cool while you are working. Without it, the difference in temperature could cause the glass to crack. The water also prevents the glass dust from escaping into the air. You do not want these particles to get into your lungs, hence the use of the water and respirator as a safety precaution.

3 Place the Mason jar on its side, cradled in a towel to prevent it from rolling around. Mark the spot on the side of the jar where you will be drilling the hole with a marker to serve as a guideline.

4 Put on your gloves, goggles, and respirator before proceeding.

5 Wet the surface of the jar. At the marked spot, begin to drill. The drill bit may slip around on the slick surface. This is normal at first. Eventually the bit will start to cut into the glass. Power up the drill as you initiate contact with the jar and keep a firm, steady hand.

6 Drilling through glass is a slow and steady process. Apply light pressure with the drill and keep the bit rotating at a slower speed. The quicker you go, the hotter the bit can get, which could potentially crack the glass. Drill for about 30 seconds and

then stop, remove the drill, and pour water over the hole. Then continue drilling some more, another 30 or 45 seconds. Stop again and spill water over the hole. Continue with this pattern. You will notice that the dust catches in the water and turns murky white. This is a good thing because it is not escaping into the air. By frequently washing down the surface of the jar, you will be removing the dust and increasing the visibility of your work area.

7   Continue drilling until you have punctured a hole all the way through the glass.

8   Wet down the surface of the jar to clean it. Safely dispose of the glass displaced by the drill. If there are any sharp edges, sand them down with sandpaper.

9   Lay out butcher paper and center your Mason jar on it. Spray-paint the jar. Allow the paint to dry.

10   Lay out the clock hands from the kit on the butcher paper. Spray-paint those with a contrasting color. Allow them to dry.

11   Follow the specific directions for putting the clock together; different kits may vary. The clock mechanism, called a movement, will go inside the jar and the threaded shaft will pass through the drilled hole. The kit should include different washers and nuts that will secure the hour, minute, and second hands to the clock movement.

12   Add super glue along the sides of the clock mechanism.

13   Insert the clock mechanism into the jar, pass the threaded shaft through the drilled hole, and press the mechanism firmly up against the glass. Hold in place while the glue dries.

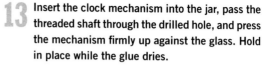

14   Attach the hour, minute, and second hands to the threaded shaft.

15   Put a battery in the clock movement and set the time.

Extra Tips

Instead of paint, try covering the Mason jar in fabric. Use a decoupage glue like Mod Podge. Coat the surface in glue, cover in fabric, and smooth out the surface. Apply a second layer of glue on top to act as a sealant.

The success of this project depends on having the correct clock kit. Some kits have short stems or shafts that will not work in a pint-size Mason jar. A longer stem is critical. The $^{15}/_{16}$-inch size fits the Mason jar perfectly. Check online at websites like Etsy and Ebay. See the Resources on page 126 for more suggestions.

See the Resources on page 126 for suggestions on where to purchase diamond drill bits.

See page 124 for a pictorial guide on successfully drilling through Mason jar glass.

Colorful & Wrapped Mini Frames

Difficulty Rating ▌▌▌

You may snap a lot of photos on your camera phone, upload them to Instagram or Facebook, and tweet your favorites on Twitter, but you probably have yet to print them out and display them in your home. These pictures tend to live digitally on phones but it does not have to remain this way. There are a variety of online print companies that will send your chosen shots to your doorstep for as little as $0.25 a print. So cull through your photos. Once your prints arrive, make these colorful mini frames to highlight your budding photography skills.

Materials

Metal bands and lids from half-pint-size Mason jars	Cotton thread, size 5, in various colors	Picture hanging strips
Butcher paper	Hot glue gun and glue sticks	Thumbtacks
White spray paint	Pencil	Ruler
Printed photographs	Scissors	Circular cork mats
	Super glue	Painter's tape
		Spray paint in various colors

1   Remove the metal bands and lids from the jars. Hang on to the jars for another craft project.

2   Lay down butcher paper outside or in a ventilated area and space out the metal bands. Coat the bands with white spray paint. Allow the paint to fully dry before proceeding. You can skip this step if you plan to completely cover your bands.

3   Take a look at the pictures you are going to use and then decide which colors of thread would be the most complimentary.

4   Dab a little bit of hot glue onto the inside of the metal band. Stick one end of thread into the glue, apply pressure, and allow to dry.

5   Begin wrapping the thread around the edge of the band. For a clean look, wrap the thread uniformly so that after each rotation the thread lines up with the previous rotation. Continue wrapping with that first color until you have desirable coverage. Add another dab of hot glue to secure the end of the thread.

6 As you work, scrunch in the thread to compress it and to help keep it uniform.

7 If you would like multicolored frames, glue a second color in place and start wrapping with that thread until you have covered more of the band. Wrap with as many colors as you like. Finish the entire band.

8 Take the metal lid and center it over one of your pictures. Printouts from Instagram or camera phone photos are the perfect size for this project. Trace the outline of the lid on the picture. Remove the lid and then cut out the circle you traced.

9 Super-glue the picture to the metal lid.

10 Apply small amounts of super glue to the edges of the metal lid and glue it down to the back of the wrapped band. Allow to bond.

11 Attach a small picture hanging strip to the back of the frame. The strip will stick to walls or other surfaces without damage. To use on a bulletin board, super-glue a thumbtack to the back of the frame.

12 To make the bulletin boards, draw out patterns with a pencil and ruler on the cork mats.

13 Apply painter's tape to the mats, covering certain areas and leaving others uncovered to receive paint.

14 Lay out the mats on butcher paper and spray-paint different sections in various colors. Allow the paint to dry. Arrange a composition of mini frames and circular bulletin boards with favorite photos and memorabilia.

Extra Tips

The small size of Instagram or camera phone pictures are ideal for this project. Many companies offer inexpensive printing of your Instagram photos. To fit these frames, print pictures at 3 inches square.

Glue thumbtacks to the back of these frames and pin them to corkboards like these circular mats. This would be a colorful and functional option for an office bulletin board.

These cork mats were found in the garden section of a local home improvement store.

Mason Night-Light

Difficulty Rating

Light up the dark, ominous corners of your home with a night-light disguised as a Mason jar. Instead of living with the ordinary plastic cover that comes with the light, replace it with something more your style, something you made yourself. This project involves drilling a hole in the glass. Take the time to follow the safety instructions laid out in this tutorial. This endeavor can be dangerous, but if you take the right precautions and equip yourself with the correct tools, this project is feasible and fairly simple.

Materials

Half-pint-size Mason jar

Drill

Marker

7/8-inch diamond drill bit

Gloves

Safety goggles

Dust mask/ particulate respirator

Watering can or hose

Sandpaper

Automatic night-light with bulb

Foam mounting tape

1. The metal lid needs to be removed for this project. The metal band is optional.

2. You will want to complete this project outside or in a garage since you will be handling glass. Set up your workspace ahead of time and make sure you are prepared before proceeding. You will need your Mason jar, a drill, a $\frac{7}{8}$-inch diamond drill bit, gloves to protect your hands, safety goggles for eye protection, and a particulate respirator to fully cover your nose and mouth. Also set up a water source. In this example, a watering can was used so that water could be repeatedly applied to the point of contact between the drill and the glass. A light stream of water from a hose would be effective as well. The water is necessary to keep the drill bit cool while you are working. Without it, the difference in temperature could cause the glass to crack. The water also prevents the glass dust from escaping into the air. You do not want these particles to get into your lungs, hence the use of the water and respirator as a safety precaution.

3. Place the mouth of the Mason jar down. You will be drilling into the bottom of the jar. Mark the spot where you wish to begin drilling with a marker. You want to position the hole as close to the back edge of the jar as possible.

4. Put on your gloves, goggles and respirator before proceeding.

5. Pour water onto the bottom of the jar. The surface is concave so it will pool up. At the marked spot, begin to drill. The drill bit may slip around on the slick surface. This is normal at first. Eventually the bit will start to cut into the glass. Power up the drill as you initiate contact with the jar and keep a firm, steady hand.

6. Drilling through glass is a slow and steady process. Apply light pressure with the drill and keep the bit rotating at a slower speed. The quicker you go, the hotter the bit can get, which could potentially crack the glass. Drill for about 30 seconds and then stop, remove the drill, and pour water over the hole. Then continue drilling some more, another 30 or 45 seconds. Stop again and spill water over the hole. Continue with this pattern. You will notice that the dust catches in the water and turns murky white. This is a good thing because it is not escaping into the air. By frequently washing down the surface of the jar, you will be removing the dust and increasing the visibility of your work area.

7. Continue drilling until you have punctured a hole all the way through the glass.

8. Wet down the surface of the jar to clean it. Safely dispose of the glass displaced by the drill. Run sandpaper along the inner face of the hole to smooth any sharp fragments.

9. Remove the plastic cover from your automatic night-light. Unscrew the bulb from the socket.

10. The plastic socket is a bit small for the hole. To prevent it from jostling, wrap foam mounting tape around the outside of the socket. The tape will form a wedge between the night-light and jar and keep it steady.

11 Insert the socket into the hole from the bottom of the jar. Screw the bulb back into the socket from inside the jar.

12 Plug in your Mason jar night-light to an electrical socket.

Extra Tips

Depending on your specific brand of automatic night-light, vary the size of the hole that you drill into the bottom of the jar. In this project, the size needed to be ⅞-inch. To determine sizing, take the automatic night-light, remove the plastic cover, unscrew the bulb, and measure the diameter of the plastic socket. Buy the drill bit that corresponds to that diameter. See the Resources on page 126 for suggestions on where to buy diamond drill bits.

Spray-paint your jar for a more colorful night-light, but avoid covering the jar in fabric or loose trims. Night-lights are not extremely hot, but you want to avoid a possible fire hazard.

Rainbow Twine Caddies

Twine, yarn, string, thread, and ribbon can often pose a challenging dilemma when it comes to organization. Long quantities of these materials are known to knot and tangle, often to the point of unbearable frustration. Avoid knotting and instead arrange your material into twine caddies. This system will minimize tangles, and twine will dispense with ease during craft projects. The glass paint used is colorful but also transparent, so the jar's contents and quantity will never be a mystery. Also the jar lids are easily removable so refilling is simple.

Materials

Pint-size Mason jars with metal bands and lids	Cardboard toilet paper rolls	1/8-inch rubber grommets
Drill	Paper towels	Butcher paper
1/8-inch drill bit	Rubbing alcohol	White spray paint
Parchment paper	Martha Stewart Liquid Fill Glass Paint	Cookie sheet
Scissors		Oven

1 With the metal bands and lids still attached to the Mason jars, drill a hole through the middle of each lid. Make sure the drill bit used is designed for metal work. Unscrew the bands and set them aside with the lids for later.

2 Prep before painting. Lay out parchment paper on your work surface. The jars need to remain undisturbed for 12 hours after painting, so choose an appropriate spot beforehand. Cut down your toilet paper rolls into 2-inch sections. The jars will be propped up on these while they dry. Soak a paper towel in rubbing alcohol and wipe down the jars. This cleans them and prepares the surface for paint.

3 Working over the parchment paper, hold the mouth of a jar in one hand and with the other, begin coating the glass with liquid fill paint. Start applying the paint below the lip of the jar, working around the jar in circles.

Paint needs to be spread over the entire surface. The paint will drip excessively down the sides onto the parchment paper. This process is a bit messy and the dripping is completely normal.

Once completely coated, prop the jar up on the cardboard roll to dry. Repeat this step for all of the jars and allow them to air-dry for 12 hours.

4 While the paint is drying, return to the metal lids. Insert the rubber grommets into the holes in the lids. Drilling can often leave jagged metal edges but the rubber will cover these up.

5 Lay out butcher paper and spray-paint the lids white. Allow the lids to fully dry.

6 Return to the jars. After air-drying, they need to bake in the oven to cure. Carefully remove the jars from the cardboard rolls and place them on a cookie sheet. Place the sheet in a cold oven and set the temperature to 350°F (180°C). Set a timer for half an hour. After 30 minutes, turn off the oven, but keep the jars in the oven until they have cooled down. This takes a few hours.

7 Remove the cool jars from the oven. Fill each jar with yarn, twine, string, or ribbon. Grab the end of the material and thread it through the hole in the metal lid. Then place the metal lid on the mouth of the jar and twist on the band.

Extra Tips

This paint needs to be rigorously shaken before use. After purchase, turn the bottles upside down and let them sit like this overnight or at least for a few hours. The color pigment will then evenly disperse throughout the bottle and provide better coverage on the jar. Shake the bottles by hand for five minutes right before painting.

This Martha Stewart line of glass paint comes in 20 different hues, so you can mix and match your favorite colors. But this brand isn't the only possibility. Look for others that offer even more colors and styles. There are even frosted glass and glitter varieties. In the paint section of your craft store, look for transparent and/or gloss enamel paints to match the jars in this example.

Framed Family Silhouettes

Difficulty Rating

Most homes are adorned with all kinds of family portraits, these photographs being among some of our most cherished possessions. But if you're looking for something new and crafty to spice up your walls, these framed silhouettes would be a fanciful detail that any DIY enthusiast will love. Each member of the family can shine on their own jar. Include grandparents, godparents, cousins, even pets—whichever members make your family special. And once you trace everyone's silhouettes, save those files on your computer. You can use them repeatedly in the future for a variety of craft projects.

Materials

Digital camera	Half-pint-size Mason jars	Super glue
Inkjet printer	Spray paint	Pencil
X-Acto knife	Craft tweezers	Large rustic frame
Cutting mat	Scissors	Teacup hooks
Butcher paper	Velvet ribbon	Paint brush
Decoupage glue		

1 First make silhouettes of each of your family members. The easiest way to accomplish this is by taking a picture of each person in profile. Upload those pictures to your computer. Use photo editing software like Adobe Photoshop to trace around the outline of each person. In Photoshop, use the lasso tool to do this. After tracing, fill in the outlines with a solid color and then lay them out on separate pages for printing. Size each profile to about 2 x 2¾ inches. This size is ideal for half-pint Mason jars.

2 Print your silhouettes. Use an X-Acto knife with a sharp blade to carefully cut out each family member's profile. Do your work on a cutting mat.

3 Turn over your silhouettes and lay them out on butcher paper. Brush on a coat of decoupage glue with a paint brush.

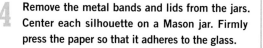

4 Remove the metal bands and lids from the jars. Center each silhouette on a Mason jar. Firmly press the paper so that it adheres to the glass.

5 Space out the Mason jars on butcher paper. Use one or more colors of spray paint to coat the jars. Allow the paint to dry before proceeding.

6 Use your X-Acto knife and craft tweezers to carefully pull up the paper silhouettes.

7 If any paint has seeped underneath the paper, you can scratch it away with an X-Acto knife to clean up the edges.

8 Cut a strip of ribbon for each jar. For this example, the ribbons were 10 inches in length, but this will vary based on your specific frame. Notch out a triangle from each end of the ribbon.

9 Super-glue each end of the ribbon to opposite sides of the Mason jar. Hold the ribbon in place for a minute while the glue dries. Repeat this for each jar. Super glue can often take a full 24 hours to fully adhere.

10 Figure out placement of the jars within the length of the frame. With a pencil, mark the center point of each jar along the inner edge of the frame.

11 Screw in a teacup hook at each center point.

12 Hang the Mason jars from the teacup hooks. Prop up or hang the frame in your home.

Extra Tips

This project would make a thoughtful gift for all kinds of people. Make a set for a recently married couple. Make up a jar of each grandchild to gift to grandparents. Even people with furry children could benefit from these family silhouette displays.

If you don't own Adobe Photoshop or something similar, try Pixlr's free online photo editor (www. pixlr.com). Its basic functions are a lot like Photoshop's. In this program, you can also use the lasso tool to trace your silhouettes.

Patchwork Butterfly Specimen Jars

Difficulty Rating ▮ ▮ ▮

Inspired by natural history museums and ento-mological exhibits, these specimen jars were designed to put your own handmade creations under glass and on display. To find vibrant butterflies, look to your own fabric scrap pile for inspiration and stitch up these magnificent insects with just a needle and thread. Pattern and color options are endless and you can create other species using the same techniques listed here. The Mason jar functions as a glass cloche, protecting your handiwork and giving it distinction.

Materials

7-inch round wood plaques	Pruning shears	26-gauge green floral wire
Butcher paper	Super glue	Wire cutters
Dark chestnut acrylic or latex paint	Scissors	Hot glue gun and glue sticks
Paint brush	Fabric scraps	Quart-size Mason jar
Wood stain	Thread	Paper
Twigs	Brown pen	Floral pins
	Needle	

1 Place the round wood plaques on top of butcher paper. Coat the plaques in a layer of paint. To achieve the color used in this example, pick a reddish-brown color like a dark chestnut. Allow plaques to dry.

2 Brush a layer of wood stain on top of the paint. The stain used in this example was antique walnut. Allow the stain to fully dry before proceeding.

3 While the plaques are drying, pick out twigs or small branches from your yard or neighborhood to use in the project. Dried-out branches work best. Use pruning shears to cut down twigs and size them appropriately to fit onto the wood plaques and underneath the Mason jar.

4 Put super glue on the bottom of the twig and glue it to the center of the wood plaque. Hold in place for a few minutes to allow the glue to dry.

5 To make the body of the butterfly, cut a scrap of light-colored fabric, like muslin or linen, to about 2½ x 5 inches. Begin rolling the fabric like you would roll a sleeping bag. As you roll, tuck in the 2 ends to round out the body. Do not worry about fabric fraying or an uneven roll. The imperfections add to the beauty of this project.

6 Begin wrapping the body with colored thread. The thread will hold the rolled fabric in place and add color to the butterfly. Once completely wrapped, cut the thread and knot it to secure.

7 To make the wings, draw out the shape of butterfly wings onto solid-colored fabric. A navy blue was used in this example. Cut out these shapes. You will need 2 wings per butterfly. If you're making

multiple butterflies, draw a template on paper and use that as your guide for each wing.

8 Cut out small, curvilinear shapes from patterned fabric to place on top of the wings. Layer patterns and colors to make the butterflies more brilliant and unique.

9 Backstitch veins running through the wings. These stitches will add texture to the wings as well as hold the pieces of fabric together. To complete a backstitch, thread a needle and tie a knot at the end. Insert the needle up through the fabric and down again to make a single stitch. Then insert the needle a space away from the previous stitch and come up through the fabric. Finally, come down with the needle, passing through the fabric at the end of the first stitch. Continue this process

in a line. Search online for photos or diagrams that show this process.

10 Stitch both wings onto the body of the butterfly. Make as many butterflies as you want.

11 Clip small pieces of floral wire to use as antennae. You will need two pieces per butterfly. Poke the wire into the fabric in the butterfly's body. Use hot glue to hold in place if necessary.

12 Hot-glue butterflies to the twigs.

13 Turn the Mason jar upside down and set it on top of the twig on the plaque.

14 To make the name tag, cut a ½ x 5-inch piece of paper. Write out papilio luminosus (meaning "colorful butterfly" in Latin) with a brown pen. Stick two floral pins in the ends of the paper and press into the wood plaque.

Extra Tips

These butterflies have a patchwork-quality and are meant to be messy. As you work with the fabric, the edges will fray and add to the character. A fray-stop solution could be used to create a cleaner edge if so desired.

Follow these same steps to make different insects. Ladybugs, grasshoppers, honey bees, or spiders are all great possibilities. You will find that these fabric versions are much friendlier than their real counterparts.

Rustic Fern Photogram Lamp

Difficulty Rating ❚ ❚ ❚

S un prints may have been something you experi-
mented with as a kid, but this artistic process
is far from juvenile. Prints made from sunlight are
known as photograms, and the results can yield
something quite sophisticated and contemporary.
Pair Lumi Inkodye light-sensitive paint with all kinds
of objects and materials to define bold silhouettes
and natural patterns. The paint is available in three
colors: red, blue, and orange. Far from limiting,
these colors can be mixed, diluted, exposed for
varying lengths of time, and applied to different
fabrics to achieve a plethora of results.

Materials

Lampshade	Disposable plate	Mason jar lamp kit, pre-wired
Scissors	Paint brush	
Linen fabric	Glass	9-inch detach-able harp
Cardboard	Washing machine	Quart-size Mason Jar with regular mouth (not wide mouth)
Thumbtacks	Laundry detergent	
Flowers or greenery	Fabric glue	Light bulb
Lumi Inkodye paint	Crescent wrench	

1. Measure your lampshade to obtain the circumference and height. The lampshade for this project was 25½ inches around and 8¼ inches tall.

2. When cutting your linen, add an allowance of 2 inches onto your measurements. For this example, the fabric was cut to 27½ x 10¼ inches.

3. Find cardboard that will cover your workspace and fit it beneath your piece of fabric. Lay out the linen onto the cardboard and pin down the corners with thumbtacks.

4. Forage in your backyard or neighborhood to find flowers or greenery that appeal to you. Remember to focus on the shape rather than the colors or texture of your clippings. Mock up your design on the fabric. Figure out the arrangement and then move pieces off to the side for the next step.

5. Complete this step in a room with low light. Shake the bottle of Inkodye paint for 1 minute. Pour out some paint onto a disposable plate. Begin painting the surface of your fabric. The paint can be applied in a messy manner, the imperfections will add to the charm and uniqueness of the piece. Apply paint to most of the fabric. A thin layer will suffice. Do not soak the material and blot away excess with a paper towel. In this example, the blue color of Inkodye was used.

6. While the paint is damp, move your flower or greenery arrangement back onto the fabric.

Remove the thumbtacks. Position a large piece of glass over the fabric and set it down on top of your design. The glass will hold the greenery in place.

7. Move the fabric outside into the sunlight. Expose the paint to light for 10 to 15 minutes. The paint will darken up during this time. The exposure time will vary depending on weather conditions.

8. Once the paint has been properly exposed, remove the glass and greenery. Machine wash the fabric with detergent in hot water to remove excess dye. After washing, allow the linen to air-dry.

9. Place the lampshade down on its side and position the linen over the shade. Add fabric glue to the top and bottom of the lampshade and press the linen down into the glue. Allow the glue to dry.

If you desire a cleaner look, fold in the frayed edges over the rim.

10 Before attaching the lamp kit to the Mason jar, use a crescent wrench to unscrew the threaded nut from the bottom of the lid. Separate the lid from the lamp mechanism.

11 Insert the base of the detachable harp between the lamp mechanism and the lid. Bring those 3 components together and screw the threaded nut back on and tighten.

12 Pop the detachable harp into place. Screw in a light bulb. Set the lampshade on top of the harp and screw in a lamp finial.

Extra Tips

Fabri-Tac is a great option for the fabric glue in this project. This glue seals very quickly and does not leave messy residue.

The Lumi Inkodye is available in three colors: blue, red, and orange. Dilute the colors with water or mix the three to achieve varied hues. Experiment on small scraps of fabric before starting a larger project.

Look beyond natural elements to imprint onto your fabric. Try lace, doilies, letters, or photo negatives, for example. Visit the Lumi website (www.lumi.co) to see how to transfer your favorite photos to fabric. This technique can be quite stunning.

Parties & Presents

MASON JAR CAKE STANDS

MINI RIBBON CHANDELIERS

PARTY PIÑATAS

PIE-IN-A-JAR WITH STAMPED MUSLIN TAG

Mason Jar Cake Stands

Difficulty Rating

Your treats will never look sweeter than when they're sitting atop these distinctive cake stands. By thrifting one-of-a-kind vintage plates and tins you can personalize these party essentials in colors that complement your style. Use plates with a pink motif for a girl's baby shower. Find red and green designs to celebrate the holidays. Remember to mix and match the Mason jars as well. Quart jars will make tall stands while half-pint jars will be short. For bite-size treats like cupcakes, make mini stands with dessert plates or saucers.

Materials

Vintage plates and tins

Mason jars of various sizes

Super glue

Butcher paper

1   Wipe down the vintage plates with a damp cloth and then allow to dry. The surface should be clean and dry before gluing.

2   Protect your work surface with butcher paper before beginning.

3   Determine which jars to pair with each vintage plate. Vary the pairings to create an eclectic mix. The glue will seal better to flat surfaces so choose plates accordingly. Consider the stability of the cake stands as you initially position the plates on top of the jars.

4 Apply super glue sparingly to the mouth of the upright Mason jar. Remember to follow all directions provided with your specific brand of glue. Position the plate over the jar and then set it down on top.

5 Lightly apply pressure to the top of the plate to ensure that a strong bond forms. Hold for about 1 minute. The glue will start to bond quickly, but let the cake stand sit overnight to ensure proper adhesion. Given the proper amount of drying time, the cake stands should be strong, durable, and washable.

6 Repeat this process to make the other stands.

Extra Tips

Leave Mason jars untreated for a clean look as seen in the example. To add more color to the project, spray-paint the jars in complementary colors before gluing to the plates. You want to avoid putting spray paint on surfaces that come into contact with food, so do not paint the plates.

For texture, consider filling the jars with small trinkets before gluing. Possible ideas include: seashells, coins, old buttons, or river rocks. Just make sure the items are not perishable.

Mini Ribbon Chandeliers

Do-it-yourself party decor doesn't need to be elaborate and tedious. In fact, an impromptu party is even easier than you think with a simple idea like this one for mini ribbon chandeliers. Their small size makes them manageable. Using supplies you have on hand, you can complete one in about 20 minutes. Group an assortment to make more of a statement and impress guests with all the frills and fringe. And once the party is over, these chandeliers look just as sweet hanging around your home.

Materials

White yarn	Scissors	Muslin fabric
Mason jar bands of various sizes	Ribbon in various materials and colors	Hot glue gun and glue sticks

1 For each chandelier, cut a 20-inch piece of yarn.

2 Take one metal band and one piece of yarn. Double-knot both ends of the yarn onto the band, placing them across from each other. Repeat this for each chandelier.

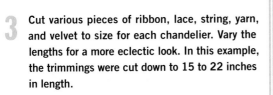

3 Cut various pieces of ribbon, lace, string, yarn, and velvet to size for each chandelier. Vary the lengths for a more eclectic look. In this example, the trimmings were cut down to 15 to 22 inches in length.

4 To make muslin strips, cut a small square of muslin the same length as your other trimmings. Along one edge, cut little incisions spaced at about ½ to 1 inch apart. Take each sliver and rip it from the muslin square. The fabric rips fairly straight and the edges look frayed and natural.

5 Take your first piece of trim, put a dab of hot glue on one end, and apply it to the inside of the metal band. The trim should come up and hang over the outside of the band. Continue this all the way around until the entire band is covered. You do not need to follow a specific pattern. Instead, place trim at random and visually compose each chandelier as you go.

6 Hang your chandeliers, grouping them for a more stunning effect.

Extra Tips

The texture of your trimmings will drastically alter the character of your chandeliers. For something sleek, use satin ribbons and metallics. For a rustic version, use burlap strips and jute twine. Translucent materials will give a soft, airy impression. Heavy cottons and colors will be bold and substantial.

A large group of these chandeliers would be impressive at a wedding. Compose a large grouping of them as a unique alter display or have them highlight the dessert table as a backdrop.

Party Piñatas

Difficulty Rating ▮▮

Piñatas conjure up images of brightly colored, fringed animals, and although the bold hues and frill are the same for this project, the results are far from average. Much smaller in size, each guest can receive their own piñata and therefore delight in their own personal stash of candy. This will surely be a party pleaser for kids and adults alike. Get creative with various edging and layering effects. Fringe scissors, pinking shears, and decorative paper punches provide all kinds of possibilities.

Materials

Scissors	Fringe scissors	Tacky glue
Crepe paper streamers in various colors	String	Pencil
	Super glue	Paint brush
Circle, triangle, and/or square paper punch	Quart-size Mason jars	Candy
	White paper	

1. Cut crepe paper streamers into 13-inch strips. Depending on the amount of layers you desire, you will need at least eight of these strips per jar.

2. With scissors and paper punches, apply various treatments to the edges of the strips. Use fringe scissors, regular scissors, and circle and triangle punches to achieve various effects.

3. Cut a 24-inch piece of string. With super glue, adhere each end of the string to the sides of the Mason jar. Allow the glue plenty of time to dry.

4. Set the Mason jar mouth down on white paper. Trace around the mouth of the jar. Cut out the circle and set aside.

5 Apply tacky glue to the edge of a strip with a paint brush. Starting at the mouth of the Mason jar, run that strip of crepe paper along the outer circumference of the jar. Press down firmly so it can adhere.

6 Continue gluing and layering crepe paper until the jar is completely covered.

7 Take the circle you cut in Step 4. Cut 2 pieces of string that have the same diameter as the circle. Glue those pieces of string to the circle in an "x" pattern using tacky glue.

8 Cut a 12-inch piece of string. Slip this string through the center of the "x" and tie a double knot. Allow the rest of the string to dangle down.

9 Fill the Mason jar with your preferred choice of candy.

10 Glue the circle with the "x" on it to the mouth of the Mason jar with tacky glue. Let the glue dry. Then carefully flip the jar over and hang as a piñata.

Extra Tips

Unlike traditional piñatas, you should avoid smashing these versions. A slight pull on the string will release the candy from inside the jar.

Stack strips of crepe paper and cut them all out at once. It is easier to cut this way and it will save you time.

Pie-in-a-Jar with Stamped Muslin Tag

Difficulty Rating ▮ ▮ ▮

If you love pie, you are sure to love pie in a Mason jar. If you can manage to give some of these delicious treats away, all you need are a few embellishments like this stamped muslin gift tag. Stamp carving is a simple technique and even beginners will find it straightforward and easy to master. A stamp carving kit will get you well on your way. Once carved, stamp all the gift tags you need. This works great for stamping in bulk, like for a wedding or large party. With this handmade tag, pie has never looked so sweet!

Materials

8 half-pint-size Mason jars

Apple pie ingredients (see recipe below)

Scissors

Muslin fabric

Hole punch

Scanner

Inkjet printer

Printer paper

Pie-in-a-Jar Template (see Template Workbook, page 121)

Tracing paper

Pencil

Stamp carving block

Wood carving handle

#4 U-shaped gouge tip

#2 V-shaped cutter tip

Black stamp pad

Velvet ribbon, twine, or mini clothespins

Vintage dessert spoons

Apple Filling Ingredients:

6 cups tart or tart-sweet apples (i.e. Granny Smith or Braeburn), about 4-5 apples

1 tbsp fresh lemon juice

½ cup sugar

½ cup packed brown sugar

2 tbsp all-purpose flour

½ tsp cinnamon

¼ tsp nutmeg

Crumble Topping Ingredients:

½ cup packed brown sugar

¼ cup all-purpose flour

½ cup rolled oats

¼ tsp cinnamon

⅛ tsp sea salt

4 tbsp unsalted butter, cut into ½-inch cubes

---

1 Core the apples and chop them up into ¼-inch cubes, keeping the skins. Put the apples in a large bowl and drizzle lemon juice over them. Set aside.

2 Combine the sugar, brown sugar, flour, cinnamon, and nutmeg in a medium bowl. Stir the ingredients until they are properly blended.

3 Pour the sugar-mixture over the apples and toss the apples with your hands. Make sure the apples are thoroughly coated.

4 In another medium bowl, combine the dry ingredients for the crumble topping: the brown sugar, flour, oats, cinnamon, and sea salt.

5 Add the butter cubes to the dry ingredients and cut in using a pastry blender or food processor until it resembles coarse crumbs.

6 Fill each of the Mason jars three-quarters full with the apple filling. Spread the crumble topping over the apple filing in each jar. With a spoon, pack in the crumble. Leave a ¼-inch of space below the rim of the jar.

7 Arrange the Mason jars on a cookie sheet. Place some aluminum foil over the top of each jar to prevent the crumble from burning. Place the cookie sheet in a cold oven. Set the temperature to 375°F (190°C). Once the oven is to temperature, bake the jars for 15 minutes. Then lower the temperature to 350°F (180°C) and bake for another 20 minutes.

8 After baking, turn off the oven but leave the Mason jars in the oven for cooling. You do not want to pull them out abruptly. Let the jars cool for 10 to 15 minutes. Then remove the jars and take off the aluminum foil. The jar contents will have shrunk a bit after baking, leaving enough room to place a hefty dollop of vanilla ice cream on top. Enjoy!

Recipe adapted from ourshareoftheharvest.com

---

1 Remove the metal bands and lids from the Mason jars. Clean the jars before proceeding with the recipe.

2 Follow the recipe to bake the mini pies in the Mason jars.

3 For each jar, cut a 2¼ x 3-inch tag of muslin and fray the edges with your fingers.

4 Punch a small hole at the top of each square of muslin. Set aside.

5 Scan the provided pie-in-a-jar template and print it out. Put the tracing paper on top of the template and trace over the outline.

6 Flip over the tracing paper and set it on top of the carving block. Trace back over the lines you drew in the last step, pressing down firmly to complete the transfer. Slowly remove the tracing paper,

making sure that everything transferred onto the block.

9 Stamp the design onto each of the muslin tags.

7 Start cutting out the block, cutting away everything other than the traced design. Use the U-shaped gouge tip for removing large chunks of the block and the V-shaped cutter tip for doing fine detailing around the design.

10 Tie the tags onto the jars with ribbon or twine or attach them with mini clothespins. Tie on spoons to the side of each jar so that these pies are all ready for eating. Add other decorative flourishes to embellish these treats.

8 Dab the stamp pad onto the cut-out design.

Extra Tips

If you are new to carving, purchase a Speedball Carving Kit (www.speedballart.com). It includes everything you need for this tutorial, including a carving block, a wood handle, a cutter and gouge tip, tracing paper, and detailed instructions.

Buy a set of alphabet stamps to mark each muslin tag with the names of family and friends.

Various pie recipes can be converted to bake in Mason jars. Use seasonal fruits and switch up your recipe throughout the year. Search recipes online to get ideas.

Weddings

CALLIGRAPHY DRINK JARS

JUTE-WRAPPED SUCCULENT FAVORS

RING BEARER PILLOW IN A JAR

TREAT JAR ESCORT CARDS

VINTAGE FORK SIGNAGE

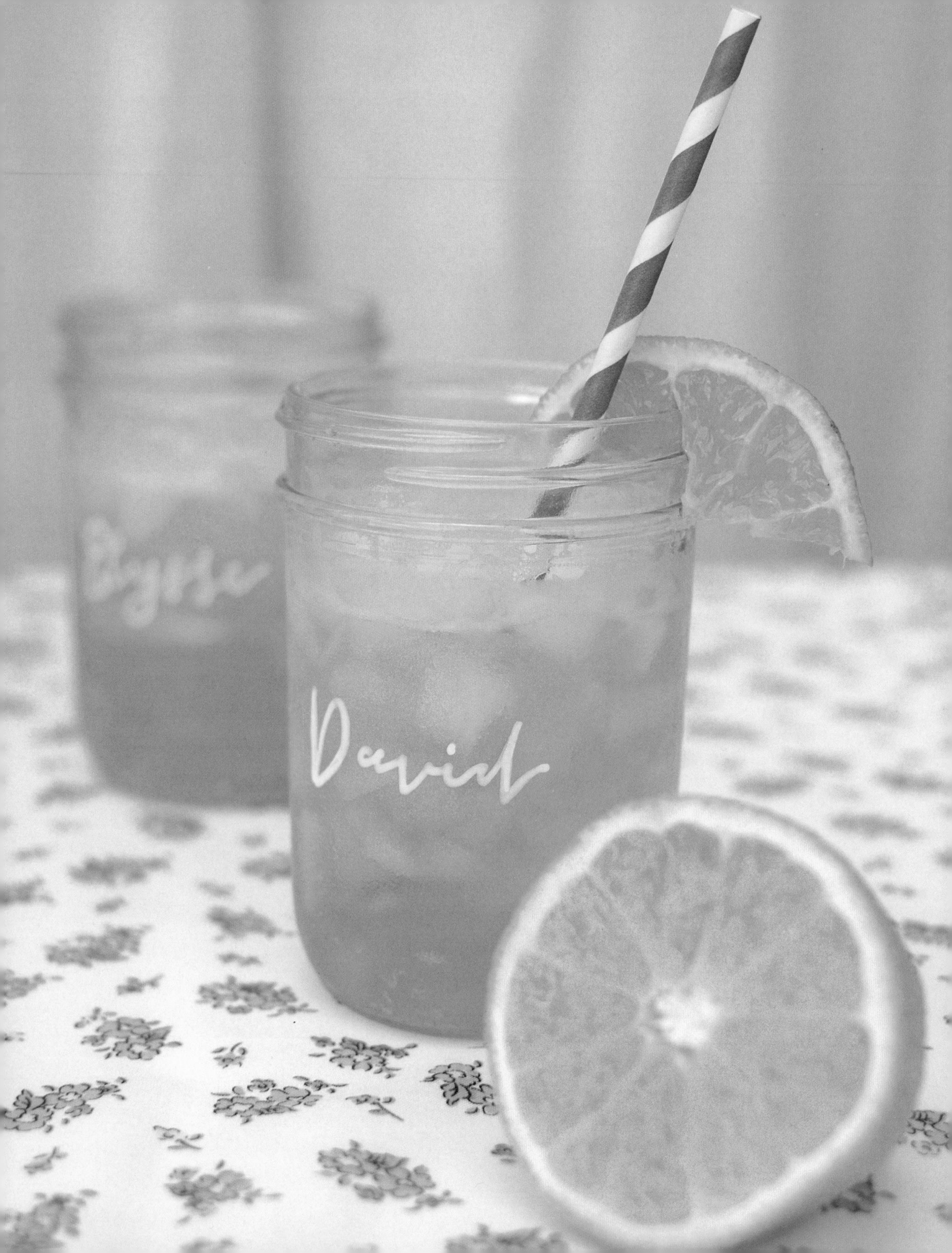
David

Calligraphy Drink Jars

Difficulty Rating ▮ ▮

Handwritten calligraphy is a personal touch that can make a wedding day extra-special for you and your guests. This distinctive detail is not only romantic but practical too. Labeled Mason jars will help guests identify their drinks throughout the night, and since they can be used repeatedly, it is an eco-friendly alternative to plastic cups. Calligraphy details are very stylish in weddings now, but not all brides can afford a personal calligrapher. This project is the perfect solution for a less expensive, DIY alternative or for the bride who lacks confidence in her own freehand writing abilities.

Materials

Inkjet printer	Pint-size Mason jars	Oven
Printer paper	Glass paint marker, white	Striped paper straws
Scissors		
Double-sided tape	Cookie sheet	*Font Used: Jacques & Gilles by Emily Lime*

1 Choose a calligraphic font that is both whimsical and legible and load it onto your computer. Graphically lay out guest's names in the chosen font using some kind of graphic software (like Adobe Photoshop or Illustrator, Microsoft Word, etc.). For pint-size jars, size the font appropriately so that names do not exceed more than 2.5 inches in width. This will ensure that names are easy to read on the curved surface of the Mason jars. Reminder: Steps 1 through 3 give direction in tracing names from an existing font. Skip these steps and write names freehand if you or someone you know is comfortable printing letters without a guide.

2 Print out guest's names, arranging a handful of names per page. Cut down each of the names individually.

3 Apply double-sided tape to the front of the name tags. Slip one into a Mason jar, position it, and press it down firmly against the glass. The double-sided tape will temporarily hold the name tag in place so that the letters can be traced over.

4 Use the glass marker to trace over the name or to write it out freehand. Remove the paper. Allow the jar to fully dry for four hours to guarantee that the paint permanently seals itself to the glass.

If using a different marker, follow the directions provided with that specific product.

5 After four hours of dry time, arrange the Mason jars on a cookie sheet and place them in a cold oven. Set the oven to 375°F (180°C). Once the oven is up to temperature, bake the jars for 40 minutes. Turn off the oven, open the door, and allow the jars to cool inside the oven when finished. Repeat Steps 4 and 5 for all of the jars.

6 Adorn drinks with paper straws to coordinate with your wedding or event and to make the jars festive.

Extra Tips

The paint on these Mason jars will need to hold up to excessive handling and condensation because they're being used as drink glasses. By allowing plenty of dry time and by baking the jars, the paint can seal itself to the glass. This will prevent chipping and smearing and leave your calligraphy looking great throughout the entire event.

Wash these jars by hand to maximize the life of the painted names. After the wedding is over, use them every day for your favorite refreshments.

Ring Bearer Pillow in a Jar

Difficulty Rating

R ing bearers have carried small pillows down the aisle for decades, taking a traditional approach in the delivery of the wedding rings. For the bride and groom who wish to see something different in their procession, this Mason jar pillow is a new variation. Young ring bearers can proudly transport this jar down the aisle and couples can appreciate this fresh take on a classic. Make a matching jar filled with petals to give to the flower girl.

Materials

Quart-size Mason jar	10-inch piece of ribbon	Block of scrap wood
5 x 3½-inch Styrofoam egg	Ruler	Large nail
Craft knife	Leather belt	Hammer
	Scissors	Jute twine
6 x 6-inch piece of linen fabric	Pencil	Fresh or dried flowers for decoration
Hot glue gun and glue sticks		

1 Remove the metal band from the Mason jar and set aside.

2 Cut the Styrofoam egg in half with a knife. Use the end that is more rounded. Drape the linen fabric over the Styrofoam and then tuck in the edges underneath it. Pull taut and hot-glue in place.

3 Glue the linen-covered Styrofoam ball into the inside of the metal band. The Styrofoam should protrude out through the top. Tighten the band back onto the jar.

4 Fold the ribbon in half to find the center point. Place a dab of glue at that point and then apply it to the top of the linen-covered Styrofoam. The rings will eventually be tied here.

5 Measure out a section of the leather belt and cut it down to 20 inches with scissors.

6 Half an inch from each end of the belt, mark a center point with a pencil. Place one end of the belt over a block of scrap wood. Line up a large nail over the dot and hammer the nail into and through the leather. Repeat this with the other end. The nail will be driven through the leather and into whatever surface is below it, hence the scrap wood to protect your work surface. Instead of a nail, you can also use a stitching awl.

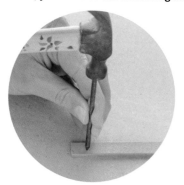

7 Cut an 18-inch piece of jute twine. Wrap the twine around the jar a couple times below the band. Pass the twine through the holes in each end of the belt. Tie a knot in the twine. Glue sections of the jute to the glass for added strength.

8 Glue fresh or dried flowers around the jar.

9 Slip wedding rings through the ribbons and tie into a bow before heading down the aisle.

Extra Tips

Inexpensive leather belts can be found at local thrift stores, Goodwill stores, or big chain stores like Target. Find one in a hue and texture that complements your wedding colors.

The flowers and colors used in this example would look great at a shabby chic, garden wedding. By switching out colors and adornments, this DIY can be customized to your specific event.

For added visual interest, fill the inside of the jar with items that correspond to your theme. For a beach wedding, fill the jar with shells or sand. For a mountain wedding, fill it with pinecones. For a vintage wedding, fill it with old spools. Get creative!

Jute-Wrapped Succulent Favors

Difficulty Rating ▯ ▯

Deciding on ideal wedding favors can be a challenge. You want them to show your gratitude as well as be valuable to your guests. Choose to make something by hand and put a little love into your gifts. Succulents are easy plants to maintain, a characteristic that any guest will highly regard. And these wrapped jars are not only rustic and full of charm but are also easy and inexpensive to make, two traits that any DIY bride will appreciate.

Materials

Half pint-size Mason jar	Jute twine	Wood skewer
Hot glue gun and glue sticks	Scissors	Scrap linen fabric
	Succulent	

1 Remove the metal band and lid from the Mason jar.

2 Place a thin line of glue along the bottom edge of the jar and then press the twine down into the glue. Apply pressure to the twine while the glue dries.

3 Repeat Step 2 to cover the entire jar, doing a little section at a time and slowly working your way up and around the Mason jar.

4 Continue wrapping until the entire jar is completely covered. Cut the twine when you have finished.

5 Plant your succulent in the jar.

6 To make the little flag, cut down a wooden skewer to 6 inches. Knot a scrap of frayed linen onto the end. A dab of hot glue will help hold it in place. Stick the flag into the jar for a simple embellishment.

Extra Tips

These jute-wrapped jars can shine in more ways than one on your wedding day. Turn them into table centerpieces or have them line your walk down the aisle. Both Mason jars and jute twine are low cost, so this DIY is ideal for a bride on a budget.

Succulents look great in your home too. Spice up any boring planters you may have for a touch of rustic beauty.

Treat Jar Escort Cards

Difficulty Rating

Direct guests to their seats in a sweet way with these Mason jar escort cards. Everyone is sure to appreciate treats to munch on throughout the night and the jar is a practical way for your guests to transport their leftovers home. Popcorn is an ideal snack. Set up a popcorn bar where guests can sprinkle their favorite toppings over their popped kernels, like butter, cheese, salt, rosemary, sugar, cinnamon, and chocolate, to name just a few. Other possibilities for filling up the Mason jars include candy, chocolates, marshmallows, cookies, or berries. Little sweets are sure to be a big hit at your wedding.

Materials

Watercolor paper or cardstock	Printer paper	Burlap
X-Acto knife	Thin paint brush	Hot glue gun and glue sticks
Scissors	Wooden skewers	Pint-size Mason jars
Metal ruler	Butcher paper	
Cutting mat	White spray paint	Popcorn or candy
Watercolor paints	Double-sided tape	*Font Used: Bombshell Pro by Emily Lime*
Inkjet printer		

1. To make the name tags, cut the watercolor paper into ¾ x 6-inch pieces. You will need one tag per guest. For precise cutting, use an X-Acto knife and metal ruler and do your work on a cutting mat. Scissors will also work.

2. Use watercolor paints to write out guest's names and table numbers on each of the tags. If you are uncomfortable with your own handwriting, choose a favorite font and layout names on the computer (use software like Adobe Illustrator or Photoshop or Microsoft Word). Print out the names and then use this as a guide while you paint.

3. Notch out a little triangle from the end of each tag with the X-Acto knife.

4. The wooden skewers should be about 10 inches long. Cut them down if necessary. Lay out the skewers on butcher paper and spray-paint them white. Turn them over and spray the opposite side. After applying full coverage allow the skewers to dry.

5. Put a strip of double-sided tape onto the end of a flag. Wrap this end around the top of a skewer and secure to the back of the flag. Repeat this for all of the flags.

6. Remove the metal bands and lids from the Mason jars.

7. Cut the burlap into 12 x 3-inch strips, one strip per jar.

8. Hot-glue one end of the burlap to the jar. Wrap the burlap around the jar and then glue down the opposite end. Repeat this for each jar.

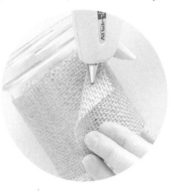

9. Fill each jar with treats along with a flag to act as a guide for guests to find their seats.

For more of a personal twist, try painting your own calligraphy or request the assistance of a talented friend.

Another option for a wedding is to use these jars as take-home favors. Instead of spelling out guests' names across the flags, write the name of the bride and groom, their initials, or their wedding date.

Olivia
Williams

Vintage Fork Signage

Difficulty Rating

Old forks can have new life again when paired with Mason jars, and they will shine as the perfect detail for rustic, vintage-inspired weddings and parties. Prominently display all types of signage to help educate and direct your guests at your venue. The fork prongs can hold name tags, table numbers, seating arrangements, food and dessert labels, photo booth directions, maps, and countless other signs and tags. Use them in your home as well to exhibit family photographs or to prop up recipes while you cook.

Materials

Inkjet printer	Metal ruler	Quart-size and pint-size Mason jars
Cardstock	Scissors	
Scanner	Cutting mat	Super glue
Signage Templates (see Template Workbook, page 120)	Stovetop	*Font Used: Nelly Script Flourish & Darling Monograms by Tart Workshop*
	Stockpot	
	Vintage forks	
X-Acto knife	Tongs	

1 Choose a decorative font and load it onto your computer. Graphically lay out table numbers, labels, guests' names, and/or signage in the chosen font using some kind of graphic software (like Adobe Photoshop or Illustrator, Microsoft Word, etc.). Start from scratch or scan the provided template and use it in your designs.

2 Print out your designs on the cardstock, arranging as many per page as possible. Cut down each of the designs individually. An X-Acto knife and metal ruler will ensure even, clean cuts, but scissors work also. If you choose to cut with an X-Acto knife, do your work on a cutting mat.

3 Boil water on your stove in a stockpot. Make sure there is enough water so that the silverware will be fully submerged. Once the water is boiling, drop the forks into the stockpot. Let them sit for about five minutes.

4 Remove the forks one at a time with the tongs.

5 Take a fork and bend it by hand in the center. Use the edge of your kitchen counter or something equivalent to help if necessary. The metal should be malleable from the hot water. Bend the fork into the shape you want.

6 Try positioning the fork on the Mason jar. Multiple points of contact with the metal and glass will ensure stability so keep this in mind. Readjust the shape of the fork to achieve the best possible result when gluing.

7 At the contact points, put a dab of super glue onto the fork. Place the fork onto the jar, applying pressure.

8 Allow plenty of time for the fork and jar to bond together. The glue may take a full 24 hours to achieve the best result. Check the instructions that came with your brand of glue. Position or prop up the jar so the spoon can properly adhere.

9 Repeat this process with multiple jars.

10 Slip the name tags, table numbers, treat labels, and your other designs between the fork prongs to prop up signage and give it prominence at your wedding, party, or event.

Extra Tips

For a more personal twist, try doing calligraphy by hand or asking a talented friend to help. Painting words and numbers with watercolors would be another artistic option.

Display these jars during the holidays. Prop up cards and photographs you receive in the mail from family and friends.

3

Olivia Williams

Kids

Animal Jar Hooks

Difficulty Rating ❙ ❙ ❙ ❙

Keeping a room organized is never an easy task for little ones, but with the right tools the process can be more enjoyable and encouraging. These colorful animal hooks will brighten up your child's room and serve as a friendly reminder to hang up backpacks, toys, and clothes. Color coordinate with bedroom decor and let your children choose their favorite animals. This will make them feel a part of the process and hopefully excite them about keeping their rooms clutter-free.

Materials

Scissors	Scrap wood	10 (½-inch) screws
Cotton fabric	Large nail	
Iron	Hammer	2 (1-hole) D-ring hangers
18 x 6-inch piece of ½-inch MDF board	Metal ruler or tape measure	4 plastic animal figurines
	Pencil	Butcher paper
Hot glue gun and glue sticks	Drill with ¹⁄₁₆-inch drill bit	Acrylic paint
4 (12-ounce) quilted jelly Mason jars with metal bands	Screwdriver	Paint brush
		Super glue

1 Cut the fabric down to about 22 x 10 inches and iron it smooth. Lay it out flat with the correct side facing down.

2 Center the piece of MDF over the fabric. Fold back the 2-inch border along one side, pulling the fabric taut and then hot-gluing it to the board. Fold each of the other 3 sides back and glue them down as well.

3 Separate the bands from the glass jars. You can discard the metal lids or save them for another time; they are not needed in this project.

4 Take the bands and turn them upside down on a piece of scrap wood. Take a large nail, position it over the band and punch a hole through the metal by hitting the nail with a hammer. Punch a second hole on the opposite side of the band. Repeat this process with all four of the bands.

5 Use a ruler and pencil to divide the fabric-covered wood into quarters. Then mark the center point of each of those 4 quarters onto the fabric.

6 Place a band over one of the marked center points. The band will have the 2 punched holes from the nail in Step 4, one on each side. Pre-drill holes into the wood in those two locations. Do this for each of the 4 bands.

7 Use a screwdriver to drill in the screws through the holes in the band and into the wood. Screw each band to the board.

8 Flip the wood board over and screw in two D-ring hangers, one on either side of the board close to the top.

9 Place the plastic animals on butcher paper. Paint each animal with acrylic paint and allow them to dry. Two or three coats may need to be applied for even coverage.

Screw the jars into their metal bands. Hang the board or prop it up for the next step.

10 Apply super glue to the feet of the plastic animals, one animal at a time. Then place the animal on the end of the jar, hold it in place, and apply pressure. The super glue may take a few minutes to start working, so continue applying pressure. Gravity will also work in your favor. Refer to the glue's directions, but it may take a full 24 hours for the plastic and glass to properly adhere together. Glue down all of the animals.

11 Hang these animal hooks on the wall. Drape bags, totes, belts, and other items from the jars as a bedroom organizer.

Instead of covering the wood in fabric, spray-paint the MDF a bright color for a monochromatic alternative.

The empty jars can serve as extra storage for your kid's small belongings. Unscrew the jars and fill them up with Legos, toy cars, blocks, stickers, or beads.

These hooks can also be transformed into something for a mature audience. Eliminate the plastic animals for a simple look with shabby chic flair. Adults can appreciate these hooks in many rooms, including bedrooms, bathrooms, and kitchens.

Apple Fabric Gift Wrap

Difficulty Rating ▮▮

Put a fresh twist on this traditional back-to-school teacher's gift and allow kids to swap out real apples for these crafty, fabric ones instead. Personalize these gifts to hold the favorite sweets of each teacher. The sealable jars can hold all kinds of homemade treats, including fresh cookies, fudge, jams, sauces, and other perishable items. Kids of all ages can help with the easy task of wrapping the jars. Monitor young children when using the hot glue gun or when decorating with wire.

Materials

Half-pint Mason jars	Clear elastic hair ties	Hot glue gun and glue sticks
Scissors	Black cardstock	Ribbon (optional)
Fabric scraps	Chalk marker	26-gauge wire (optional)

1. Unscrew the lid from a half-pint Mason jar and fill it with candy, baked goods, or other small treats. Reseal the lid.

2. Cut the fabric into a 12-inch square.

3. Lay the fabric out flat. Unless the fabric is double-sided, have the patterned side facing down and the back of the fabric facing up. Place the Mason jar at the center of the fabric square.

4. Draw up all 4 of the fabric corners above the top of the jar.

Gather in the excess fabric and secure it with a hair tie.

5 Draw a leaf shape onto cardstock and then cut out the shape. Use the chalk marker to spell out your gift recipient's name.

6 Dab some hot glue onto the end of the leaf tag and attach it to the top of the wrapped jar.

7 Add ribbons or wire for flourish, if using, and give to favorite teachers or friends at school.

Extra Tips

This project makes for an excellent packaging option for teacher's gifts but these apples aren't just for the classroom. Wrap up your favorite fall sweets as presents for friends and family too. Having an autumn wedding? These wrapped apples would make a great take-home favor for your guests and an easy DIY for brides and grooms to complete before the big day.

Quilted Balloon Mobile

Difficulty Rating

Hot air balloons evoke feelings of whimsy and adventure in adults and children alike. This hand-stitched, quilted version will have great appeal with young thrill seekers who can fantasize about their favorite stuffed animals sailing up into the skies. With the right colors and patterns, these mini balloons will fit right into the bedrooms of both boys and girls. Looking for party ideas? Throw a flying-themed party and hang these balloons as part of the decorations. Balloons, kites, blue skies, clouds, airplanes, these are all ideas that small adventurers will love.

Materials

- 11-inch paper lantern
- Scanner
- Hot Air Balloon Diagram Template (see Template Workbook, page 122)
- Inkjet printer
- Printer paper
- Scissors
- Fabric pins
- Patterned fabric
- Thread
- Needle
- Hot glue gun and glue sticks
- Yarn
- Half-pint-size Mason jar with metal band

1 Put together your lantern. The lantern should come with a wire frame that fits inside to give it shape.

2 Scan the Balloon Fabric Template and print it out. This template is designed specifically for an 11-inch lantern. If your lantern is a different size, refer to the notes below for making your own template. Cut out the template.

3 Pin the paper template to the fabric and cut out the shape. For this example, 4 fabrics were used. Cut out 9 fabric templates in the various patterns.

4 Determine how you want the different pieces to come together, which patterns and colors to place next to each other. Take 2 fabric templates and pin them together. The correct sides of the fabric should be facing each other, the backsides facing you.

5 Thread a needle, tie a knot at the end, and sew a running stitch along one edge. A ¼-inch seam

allowance was factored into the template. Remove the pins when finished. To complete a running stitch, pass your needle up through the fabric and then back down again next to where you just came up. Leave a bit of space and come up again with your needle and then back down. Repeat this process all along the edge of the fabric. Search online for visual diagrams to help with this stitch.

6 Take the next fabric template and pin it to one of the templates sewn in the last step. Once again, pin the fabric so that the correct sides are facing each other. Repeat these steps until all of the templates are sewn together to form a quilted cover.

7 The cover for the lantern is almost finished. Wrap the lantern in the cover and position it correctly. Pin the 2 loose ends to close up the cover around the lantern. Stitch up that last edge with a running stitch.

8 Place a little bit of hot glue along the edges of the fabric. Then tuck those ends into the openings at the top and bottom of the lantern.

9 Cut yarn in various lengths to drape from the bottom of the lantern. Loop and knot the yarn around the wire frame.

10 Wrap a piece of yarn around the lip of the Mason jar and knot it tight. From here, attach 2 pieces of yarn on either side of the jar and connect each of those ends to the wire frame in the lantern. The jar should now be able to hang from the lantern.

11 Attach yarn to the top of the wire frame so that the balloon mobile can hang freely. Display small stuffed animals in the balloon's jar basket.

Extra Tips

This project would be a wonderful baby shower gift for a new mother-to-be. Choose fabric and yarn with pink or blue motifs.

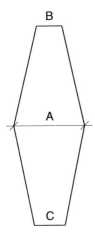

If your lantern is sized differently than the one in this example, you will need to make your own template. You will need three different measurements to do this. Put together your lantern and get a tape measure. First, measure the circumference at the middle of the lantern. Take that measurement and divide it by the number of fabric sections you will have. In this example there were nine. This calculation will be measurement A in the diagram below. Measure the diameter of the top opening in the lantern. Multiply that number by 3.14 (π) to get the circumference and then divide that number by the number of sections. This calculation will be measurement B in the diagram. Measure the diameter of the bottom opening in the lantern. Multiply that number by 3.14 and then again divide that by the number of sections. This calculation will be measurement C in the diagram. Draw out your shape. This template is sized perfectly to your specific lantern.

Piggy Bank Jar

Difficulty Rating ▮▮

The piggy bank is a classic childhood keepsake used as a tool to impart the value of money. This pink piggy will not only teach kids useful money-saving habits but also creatively inspire them since this is a project they can make for themselves. Papier mâché can be messy but budding artists will have a lot of fun getting their hands dirty. Just remember to protect your work surface and have kids wear aprons as a precaution.

Materials

Scissors	Quart-size Mason jar with band	Erasable fabric marking pen
Pink crepe paper streamer	2 wine corks	Hot glue gun and glue sticks
Butcher paper	Pink, white, and black felt	Pink pipe cleaners
Paint brush		
Decoupage glue		

1 Remove the lid from the quart-size Mason jar but keep the metal band and set it aside.

2 Take 2 wine corks and cut each in half. Hot-glue these 4 pieces to the side of the jar. These will be the feet and base for the pig. Position them so that the pig will be stable.

3 Cut the crepe paper into small pieces about 2 inches wide. The squares do not need to be perfect.

4 Cover your work surface with butcher paper. Brush a coat of decoupage glue onto a square of crepe paper and then stick it to the jar. Continue this process until a single layer of crepe paper covers the entire jar. Wrap the wine corks too. Let this layer dry thoroughly. Come back later and patch up sparse areas.

5 Draw shapes for the eyes, ears, and nose onto the felt with the erasable fabric marker. Draw the eyes and nose onto the black felt. Draw the ears onto the pink and white felt. Cut out these shapes.

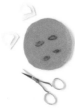

6 Cut out a 4-inch circle from the pink felt. Cut a small slit for the mouth. Make sure it is large enough for coins and folded bills to pass through.

7 Place the felt circle over the mouth of the jar and screw on the metal band to hold it in place.

8 Hot-glue the white part of the ears to the pink part and then hot-glue both to the head of the pig. Hot-glue the eyes below the ears. Finally hot-glue the nostrils just above the mouth opening.

9 To make the tail, curl a pink pipe cleaner and glue it to the back of the pig.

10 Pass coins and bills through the mouth of the pig. Unscrew the band to access the money.

Extra Tips

Use different colors of crepe paper and felt to create various animals. Use a brown color scheme and round out the ears to make a bear. Cut long, floppy ears and use a cotton ball to make a bunny.

Once the glue is dry, have kids write out their names with a marker on the side of the pig.

Insect Observatory Terrariums

Difficulty Rating ▮ ▮

Children's curiosity often attracts them to the natural world. A magnifying glass in hand, they run around the yard thoroughly investigating the flora and fauna that make up their encompassing environment. Encourage this inquisitive spirit in your children by making these insect observatory terrariums, and before long your young entomologists will have a whole new understanding and appreciation of bugs.

Materials

Quart-size Mason jar	Scissors	Wood branch
Gray fiberglass screen	Hot glue gun and glue sticks	Leaves, moss, pebbles, and natural trimmings
Pencil	Leather belt	
	Super glue	

1 Remove the metal band and lid from the Mason jar. Take the metal lid, place it on the fiberglass screen, and trace the circle with a pencil.

2 Cut out the circle traced in Step 1.

3 Turn over the metal band. Apply hot glue along the edges of the screen circle. Place the circle into the band and apply pressure.

4 Screw the band back onto the Mason jar.

5 Fasten the belt into its first notch.

6 Working in small sections at a time, apply super glue along the inside of the belt.

7 Join the belt and jar together, apply pressure, and hold in place for at least a minute so that the glue can take hold. Position the belt so that the metal buckle is not coming into contact with the glass. Continue gluing the belt around the jar. The glue may take a full 24 hours to permanently bond.

8 Unscrew the band and fill the inside with branches, leaves, moss, pebbles or any other insect necessities. Replace the band back on the jar after finding a bug and introducing it to its new home.

Extra Tips

This is a great time to teach children about humane treatment of other living creatures. Although the insects will have fresh air from the screened lid, water and food sources may be lacking in your jar ecosystem. Once children have thoroughly observed their specimens, release insects back into their natural environments.

Snap pictures or have children draw sketches of their insects before returning them to nature. These mementos will remind them of their outdoor explorations.

Maybe you wish to observe other living organisms in your glass terrarium, something other than insects. Plant moss or small plants into the jar and hang the terrarium near a bright window. You can water plants through the screened lid or remove it for routine maintenance.

Painted Animal Jars

Difficulty Rating

Serve up sweets to youngsters in these amiable jars decorated with some of the most beloved animals: a fox, tiger, and rabbit. Switch up colors to correspond to different holidays or occasions. Pastel jars look great at Easter. Gray, black, and orange are festive at Halloween time. For a birthday party, choose paints in the same colors as the decor. Remember to mix and match simple shapes to come up with other animal variations and to make your child's favorite.

Materials

Pencil	Butcher paper	Craft tweezers
8½ x 11-inch paper and/ or cardstock	Paint brush	Scissors
X-Acto knife	Decoupage glue	Hot glue gun and glue sticks
Metal ruler	Pint-size Mason jars	Candy, treats
Cutting mat	Spray paint in various colors	

1. Using basic shapes, draw out the faces of a fox, tiger, rabbit, or any other favorite animals on paper. Use an X-Acto knife and metal ruler to cut out these face shapes. Do your work on a cutting mat.

2. Cover your work surface with butcher paper. Turn over the shapes and brush on a coat of decoupage glue.

3. Arrange the shapes on the jars. Gently apply pressure so that the paper adheres to the glass and forms a strong bond.

4. Take the jars outside for spray-painting. Again, protect your work surface with butcher paper. With the jar mouth facing down, spread out the jars and lightly mist them with a coat of spray paint. Hold the can about 12 inches away from the jar and spray in a back-and-forth motion to get even coverage. Allow the paint to dry for 10 to 15 minutes.

5. Carefully peel up the paper or cardstock shapes using an X-Acto knife and craft tweezers. Some paper may stick, so use the knife to scrape it off the glass.

6. For each jar, cut out six ⅛ x 2-inch strips of paper or cardstock. Use sharp scissors to curl the ends of the paper.

7. Hot-glue the curls to the animals' faces to act as whiskers.

8. Fill the jars with candy or treats and give to children for Easter, Halloween, or other special occasions.

Extra Tips

There are alternatives to using paper and decoupage glue. Choose a material that already has an adhesive backing, for example craft vinyl, contact paper, or even sticker labels.

Place tealight candles inside each jar to create glowing animal lanterns. Line your walkway or sidewalk with these jars for a fun Halloween decoration.

Make handles for these jars out of thick craft wire, like 12-gauge, which will be strong enough to support the weight of the jar. This can be a substitute for an Easter basket or a Halloween candy bucket.

Holidays

Cranberry Christmas Display

Difficulty Rating

Mailboxes can become quite full during the holidays, often bursting with cards and photographs from loved ones. Put the spotlight on your favorites with these simple cranberry displays. Arrange them across a mantle or table to give them prominence in your home. Cranberries are just one possibility; try any variety of holiday trim like pinecones, pine needles, cinnamon sticks, jingle bells, fake snow, or small ornaments.

Materials

Mason jars
of various sizes

Christmas cards
and photographs

Fresh
cranberries

1 Remove the metal lid and band from a Mason jar.

2 Lightly bend a Christmas card to slip into the mouth of the Mason jar. Push the card up against the glass.

3 While holding the card in place, fill the jar with cranberries. As the jar gets fuller, the cranberries will keep the card in place for you.

4 Fill completely full and repeat the previous steps for multiple jars.

Extra Tips

Use these displays throughout the holiday season to hold cards and family photographs. The cranberries will keep for months. Swap out the display as new cards come in to keep things fresh.

Use this same idea to decorate at other holidays. For example, replace the cranberries with candy hearts at Valentine's Day, with pinecones at Thanksgiving, or with candy corn at Halloween.

Nestle tealights in the cranberries to light up each jar.

Jar Advent Calendar

Difficulty Rating ❚❚

Christmas advents come in all shapes and forms, ranging from the minimal to the extravagant. No matter how you celebrate that countdown to Christmas, an advent calendar is a friendly and festive reminder. This crafty version is quite versatile. Make new arrangements each year by configuring the jars differently, placing them somewhere new, or by filling them with different treats and displays. For uniformity, use jars that are all the same. For variety, mix and match as many jars as you like. Each of the 25 Mason jars is an opportunity to create something new.

Materials

Inkjet printer	Double-sided tape	Glass paint marker, white
Printer paper		
Scissors	25 Mason jars of various sizes	*Font Used: Futura by Adobe*

1 Use computer software to layout and appropriately size the numbers 1 through 25. Adobe Photoshop or Illustrator, Microsoft Word, or even Google Documents are all options. Size the numbers based on the specific jars you plan to use. Print out these numbers and roughly cut out each of them.

2 Put 2 pieces of double-sided tape on the front of the number. Slip the number into one of the jars and press it to the glass. Apply enough pressure so that it will stick.

3 Trace the number onto the glass using the white paint marker. Allow the paint to dry. If you would like the paint to permanently seal to the jars, you can bake them in the oven (follow Steps 4 and 5 in the tutorial for Calligraphy Drink Jars on page 65).

4 Repeat Steps 2 and 3 on all of the jars.

5 Arrange the jars to create a winter composition using favorite heirlooms or Christmas decorations to make the scene festive.

Extra Tips

Place little gifts or treats inside each of the jars for your family to enjoy as they count down to Christmas.

Instead of presents, fill each jar with small trinkets and compose a winter wonderland scene. Use things like bottle brush trees, plastic deer or other figurines, fake snow, candy canes, or pinecones.

You can skip Steps 1 and 2 if you feel comfortable writing out the letters freehand or allow kids to write the numbers.

Cross-Stitch Nordic Ornaments

Difficulty Rating ▮ ▮ ▮

Nordic designs are often knit into cozy blankets, warm sweaters, and festive stockings. The iconic patterns feature snowy scenes, the animals and natural elements give a nod to the beauty of winter. Your holiday may or may not include snow, but the snowflakes, pine trees, and reindeer that signify the season can still brighten up your home. Cross-stitch is a simple way to reinterpret classic Nordic knits and this project is an easy way to make new ornaments.

Materials

Scanner	Scissors	Mason Jar metal bands and lids
Nordic Templates (see Template Workbook, page 123)	White 14-Count Aida fabric	Pencil
	3-inch embroidery hoop	Hot glue gun and glue sticks
Inkjet Printer	Red embroidery floss	Red and/ or gold ribbon
Printer paper	Embroidery needle	

1. Scan the Nordic Templates into your computer and print them out to use as a guide for cross- stitching.

2. Cut a 5-inch-square piece of Aida fabric. Loosen the screws on the embroidery hoop and separate the two sections. Center the Aida fabric over the inner hoop and then place the outer hoop on top. Firmly press down to sandwich the fabric between the two. Tighten the screw and pull the fabric taut.

3. Cut a 12-inch piece of embroidery floss and separate out 2 of the 6 strands or plies. Take the 2 plies and thread one end through the needle.

4. Begin the pattern in the upper left corner and work from top to bottom, left to right. In cross-stitch, you make an "x" stitch. Complete one line at a time. When stitching a line, do all the diagonals from bottom-left to top-right first and then come back and complete the "x" with the diagonals from bottom-right to top-left.

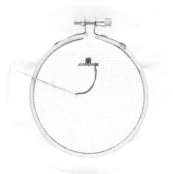

Tip: When starting with a new thread, do not knot the end. Instead hold the end in place on the back of your pattern and pass a few stitches over it to secure. When you finish with the thread, pass the needle under completed stitches and cut off the excess.

5. Complete the first design and then cross-stitch the other 2 designs on separate pieces of Aida fabric.

6. Take a metal lid and center it over each of the embroidered designs. With a pencil, trace the outline of this circle. Cut out these circles.

7. Hot-glue the embroidered designs into the backs of the metal bands. The bands will act as frames for your handiwork.

8. Hot-glue the metal lids into the metal bands as a backer. The fabric should be sandwiched between the two.

9 Cut ribbon, make a loop, and hot-glue it to the top of the band for hanging.

These ornaments would also make unique gift toppers or tags for holiday treats.

Cross-stitch is a simple technique and easy enough for beginners to learn. If you are new to cross-stitch, watch YouTube videos to pick up the basics. After a few practice runs, you can master these designs as well as many others.

Embroidered Jar Ornaments/Tags

Difficulty Rating ▐ ▐ ▐

You may not be able to hang actual Mason jars from your Christmas tree this holiday, but by making these embroidered versions, this beloved jar can still make a festive appearance in your decor. This is a simple project for those with or without embroidery experience, the backstitch being the most basic stitch to master, and the project size is ideal for beginners who might get overwhelmed by intricate patterns. Other than an ornament, these embroidered jars can be used as gift tags or toppers for holiday presents. Pair the tags with simple kraft paper and red and white baker's twine for a crafty packaging alternative.

Materials

Scanner	Muslin fabric	Felt
Mason Jar Template (see Template Workbook, page 122)	Pencil and/or erasable fabric marker	Fabric glue
		Red ribbon
Inkjet printer	Scissors	Small trinkets (like buttons, vintage millinery supplies, etc.)
	Embroidery floss	
Printer paper	Embroidery needle	

1. Scan the provided templates and then print them out. Trace the template onto a 2 x 3-inch piece of muslin fabric with a pencil or an erasable fabric marker. You may need to hold the template and muslin up to a light source, like a window, to successfully trace the lines.

2. Cut an 18-inch piece of black embroidery floss and separate out 2 of the 6 strands or plies. Take the 2 plies and thread one end through the needle, knotting the opposite end.

3. Using a simple backstitch technique, embroider the outline of the Mason jar. Embroider over all of the lines you traced. When you run out of embroidery floss, thread 2 more of the strands from Step 2 through the needle and keep going. To complete a backstitch, insert the needle up through the fabric and down again to make a single stitch. Then insert the needle a space away from the previous stitch and come up through the fabric. Finally, come down with the needle, passing through the fabric at the end of the first stitch. Continue this technique all along your Mason jar outline. Search online for photos or diagrams that show this process.

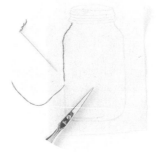

Tip: If you are making a gift tag, write out your gift recipient's name with the pencil or marker and then embroider over that. For variety, use embroidery floss of a different color.

4 Cut a 2 x 3-inch piece of felt. Turn the muslin over and place fabric glue along the underside of the embroidery and then place the felt on top of the muslin. Press together. Allow the glue a few minutes to dry. You may want to apply even pressure to the fabric by placing it underneath a heavy book.

5 Trim down the excess fabric, cutting around the outline of the embroidered jar. Leave about ⅛-inch edge around the needlework.

6 Cut a small piece of ribbon about 5 inches long. Glue the two ends together, forming a loop. Then glue this loop to the back of the embroidered jar to make a handle.

7 If you are making an ornament, hot-glue or stitch small trinkets to the front of the jar to add holiday flourish and color. Millinery pieces like gold leaf, holly, or red berries are excellent options.

Extra Tips

Follow these same steps to make a different piece of holiday decor. Stitch the numbers 1 through 25 on separate jars to make an advent calendar. Glue the Mason jars to a piece of twine and hang the advent calendar as a garland.

These embroidered Mason jars are not exclusive to holiday festivities. Use them as a handmade detail for a shabby-chic wedding. Stitch guest's names onto the jars and turn these ornaments into escort or place cards instead. Or embroider the Mason jar and the couple's initials onto muslin bags to make unique packaging for take-home favors.

Search Etsy for affordable millinery pieces if you don't have access to anything local.

Glass Bell

Difficulty Rating

The harmonious chime of a bell is a sound that has been synonymous with holidays and special occasions for years. Church bells, jingle bells, and wedding bells all mark important events. As the ringing commences, so too should the festivities. Start your own melodic traditions with a glass bell made from a Mason jar. Just a few materials are required and the simple construction is part of the beauty of this project. Remember, this DIY involves drilling a hole in the glass. Take the time to follow the safety instructions laid out in this tutorial. This endeavor can be dangerous, but if you take the right precautions and equip yourself with the correct tools, this project is feasible and fairly simple.

Materials

Half-pint-size Mason jar	Safety goggles	Scissors
Drill	Dust mask/ particulate respirator	Sandpaper
¼-inch diamond drill bit		Rope
Gloves	Watering can or hose	1-inch wooden beads
	Marker	

1 Remove the metal band and lid from the Mason jar.

2 You will want to complete this project outside or in a garage since you will be handling glass. Set up your workspace ahead of time and make sure you are prepared before proceeding. You will need your Mason jar, a drill, a ¼-inch diamond drill bit, gloves to protect your hands, safety goggles for eye protection, and a particulate respirator to fully cover your nose and mouth. Also set up a water source. In this example, a watering can was used so that water could be repeatedly applied to the point of contact between the drill and the glass. A light stream of water from a hose would be effective as well. The water is necessary to keep the drill bit cool while you work. Without it, the difference in temperature could cause the glass to crack. The water also prevents the glass dust from escaping into the air. You do not want these particles to get into your lungs, hence the use of the water and respirator as a safety precaution.

3 Set the Mason jar down with the bottom facing up. Mark the spot where you will be drilling with a marker. This mark should be in the center.

4 Put on your gloves, goggles, and respirator before proceeding.

5 Wet the surface of the jar. The bottom is concave so the water will pool up. At the marked spot, begin to drill. The drill bit may slip around on the slick surface. This is normal at first. Eventually the bit will start to cut into the glass. Power up the drill as you initiate contact with the jar and keep a firm, steady hand.

6 Drilling through glass is a slow and steady process. Apply light pressure with the drill and keep the bit rotating at a slower speed. The quicker you go, the hotter the bit can get, which could potentially crack the glass. Drill for about 30 seconds and then stop, remove the drill, and pour water over the hole. Then continue drilling some more, another 30 or 45 seconds. Stop again and spill water over the hole. Continue with this pattern. You will notice that the dust catches in the water and turns murky white. This is a good thing because it is not escaping into the air. By frequently washing down the surface of the jar, you will be removing the dust and increasing the visibility of your work area. Continue drilling until you have punctured a hole all the way through the glass.

7 Wet down the surface of the jar to clean it. Safely dispose of the glass displaced by the drill. If there are any sharp edges sand them down with some sandpaper.

8 Cut a piece of rope 20 inches long. Make a double overhand knot in the rope. To do this, first form a loop.

Next pass the end of the rope through the loop.

Then pass the end of the rope through the loop again.

Pull both ends of the rope to tighten the knot.

Before the knot is tight, slip the end of the rope through the knot to make another loop. Fully tighten the knot.

9 Pass the opposite end of the rope through the hole in the jar. Then tie a double knot to prevent the jar from slipping.

10 The remaining rope should dangle freely in the jar. Cut any excess rope if necessary. At the end tie on a wooden bead or 2 and knot to secure.

Extra Tips

Because these bells are made of glass, you want to be careful when using them. Mason jars are incredibly strong though. The wooden bead can strike the glass without causing problems.

Hang these bells outside for a unique take on wind chimes.

See page 124 for a pictorial guide on successfully drilling through Mason jar glass.

Simple Holiday Candelabra

Difficulty Rating ▌ ▌ ▌ ▌

Spending the holidays by candlelight is quite a magical way to take in the season. The flickering glow brings warmth to a room, creating a cozy and inviting atmosphere. Share your own special moments by candlelight, the bright luster radiating from your own handmade candelabra. Group jars together for a statement piece, or position single ones throughout your home for small, festive moments. Adorn jars with your favorite ribbons, twine, ornaments, or millinery to make them your own. Remember, this project involves drilling a hole in the glass. Take the time to follow the safety instructions laid out in this tutorial. This endeavor can be dangerous, but if you take the right precautions and equip yourself with the correct tools, this project is feasible and fairly simple.

Materials

Quart, pint, and half-pint-size Mason jars	Dust mask/ particulate respirator	Sheer gold wire ribbon
Drill	Watering can or hose	Hot glue gun and glue sticks
¼-inch diamond drill bit	Marker	5-inch taper candles
Gloves	Sandpaper	Scissors
Safety goggles	Butcher paper	X-Acto knife
	White spray paint	

1. Remove the metal bands and lids from the Mason jars.

2. You will want to complete this project outside or in a garage since you will be handling glass. Set up your workspace ahead of time and make sure you are prepared before proceeding. You will need your Mason jars, a drill, a ¼-inch diamond drill bit, gloves to protect your hands, safety goggles for eye protection, and a particulate respirator to fully cover your nose and mouth. Also set up a water source. In this example a watering can was used so that water could be repeatedly applied to the point of contact between the drill and the glass. A light stream of water from a hose would be effective as well. The water is necessary to keep the drill bit cool while you work. Without it, the difference in temperature could cause the glass to crack. The water also prevents the glass dust from escaping into the air. You do not want these particles to get into your lungs, hence the use of the water and respirator as a safety precaution.

3. Place the mouth of the Mason jar down. You will be drilling into the bottom of the jar. Mark the center of each jar with a marker.

4. Put on your gloves, goggles, and respirator before proceeding.

5. Work on one jar at a time. Pour water onto the bottom of the first jar. The surface is concave, so it will pool up. At the marked spot, begin to drill. The drill bit may slip around on the slick surface. This is normal at first. Apply pressure and eventually the bit will start to cut into the glass. Power up the drill as you initiate contact with the jar and keep a firm, steady hand.

6. Drilling through glass is a slow and steady process. Apply light pressure with the drill and keep the bit rotating at a slower speed. The quicker you go, the hotter the bit can get, which could potentially

crack the glass. Drill for about 30 seconds and then stop, remove the drill, and pour water over the hole. Then continue drilling some more, another 30 or 45 seconds. Stop again and spill water over the hole. Continue with this pattern. You will notice that the dust catches in the water and turns murky white. This is a good thing because it is not escaping into the air. By frequently washing down the surface of the jar, you will be removing the dust and increasing the visibility of your work area.

7 Continue drilling until you have punctured a hole all the way through the glass.

8 Wet down the surface of the jar to clean it. Safely dispose of the glass displaced by the drill. If there are any sharp edges, sand them down with sandpaper. Follow Steps 3 through 8 on the other 2 jars.

9 Lay out butcher paper to protect your work surface and spread out the 3 jars. Spray-paint the jars white. Allow the paint to thoroughly dry.

10 Group the 3 jars together, jar mouths facing down. Wrap a piece of the gold ribbon around the 3 jars, approximately in the center. Pull the ribbon taut and hot-glue in place.

11 Cut a piece of ribbon. Form a loop by gluing one end of the ribbon to the center.

12 Make a second loop, gluing the other end into the center as well.

13 Cut another small piece of ribbon and wrap it around the center point of the 2 loops. Hot-glue this bow onto the front of the candelabra.

14 Place a candle atop each jar. If it is a tight squeeze into the hole, shave off some of the wax at the bottom of the taper with an X-Acto knife.

Extra Tips

Depending on your specific candles, vary the size of the hole that you drill. In this example, the candles had a ¼-inch diameter. Measure your own and choose a drill bit accordingly. See the Resources on page 126 for suggestions on where to buy diamond drill bits.

For a rustic take on the Hanukkah menorah, group nine Mason jars together instead of three.

See page 124 for a pictorial guide on successfully drilling through Mason jar glass.

Final Table Number

Pie-in-a-Jar

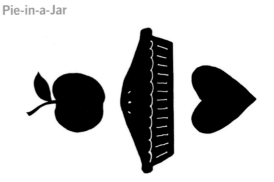

Hello Light Example – enlarge by 300%

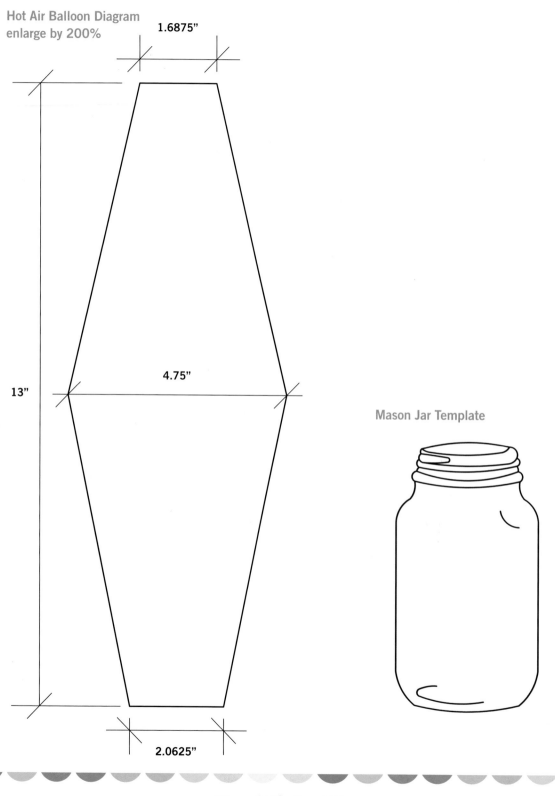

Hot Air Balloon Diagram
enlarge by 200%

1.6875"

13"

4.75"

2.0625"

Mason Jar Template

Nordic Reindeer

Nordic Snowflake

Nordic Tree

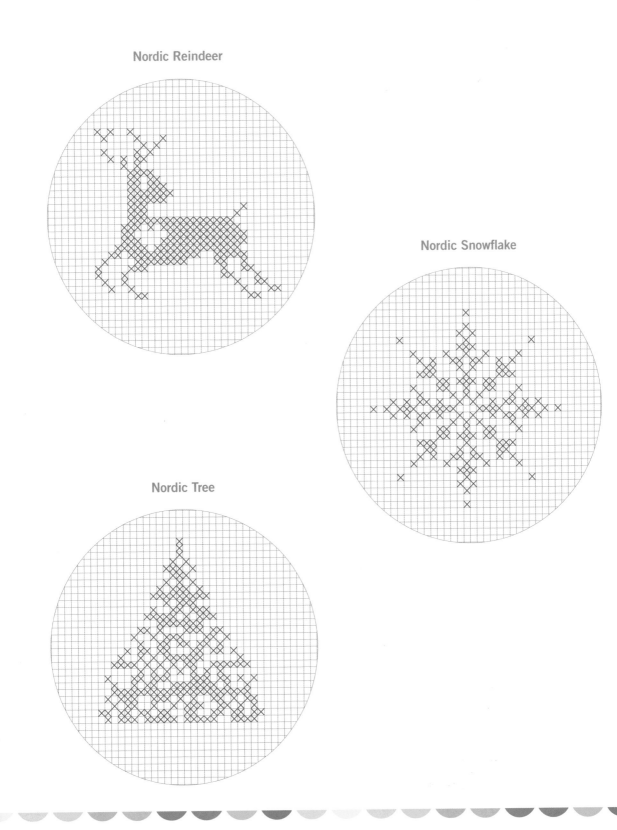

1 Cradle the Mason jar in a towel. Mark the point where you will begin drilling.

2 Wet down the surface of the jar.

3 Steady the jar with one hand and begin to drill at the marked location. The drill bit will slip around on the slick surface of the jar, but if you apply pressure, eventually the bit will cut into the glass.

4 After drilling for 30 to 45 seconds, remove the bit and pour water over the hole. This will clean away the murky water and make it easier to see your progress.

5 Insert the drill back into the groove that has been cut into the glass. Continue drilling for another 30 to 45 seconds. Then again, remove the drill and wash down the surface with water. Continue with this pattern in a slow and steady manner.

6 Continue drilling until you have punctured a hole all the way through the glass.

7 Follow all of the directions for each of the four projects that involve drilling through glass. These projects can be dangerous but if you take the right precautions and equip yourself with the correct tools, drilling through glass is a feasible and simple technique. Here are some ideas to get your started with glass drilling: Mason Clock, page 29, Mason Night-Light, page 35, Glass Bell, page 113, Simple Holiday Candelabra, page 117.

Resources

Mason jars and the materials for these crafts can be found at the following stores:

Fresh Preserving Store
www.freshpreservingstore.com

Home Depot
www.homedepot.com

Michaels
www.Michaels.com

Joann Fabrics
www.joann.com

Hobby Lobby
www.hobbylobby.com

Lowes
www.lowes.com

Amazon
www.amazon.com

Fabric paint:
Lumi
www.lumi.co

Etsy.com
www.etsy.com

Clock mechanism kit:
Brazzco Timeless Memories
www.etsy.com/shop/brazzco

Martha Stewart
shop.marthastewart.com

Striped paper straws:
Shop Sweet Lulu
www.shopsweetlulu.com

Acknowledgments

Getting the chance to develop, write, style, and photograph my first book has been a dream come true. As a little girl I constantly imagined myself growing up to be a writer. I feel so fortunate to work in a time when sharing beautiful images and vibrant stories is so effortless. I am constantly inspired by fellow photographers, stylists, crafters, and bloggers. It is a joy to do what I do.

First, I would like to thank Ulysses Press for entrusting this book to me and taking a chance on a young blogger. This has been such a wonderful collaboration and your kindness and guidance is deeply appreciated by this first-time author. I could not have imagined a better editor in Kelly Reed. Kelly, thank you so much for your support. From our first interactions, I felt so strongly about this project and our ability to put together something special.

All my love to my Grandma Flora and Aunt Ruth who introduced me to Mason jars years ago. You two have played such a large part in my creative development and I cannot thank you enough for the loving environment you provided for David and me. You are responsible for so much of who I am today, but most importantly you instilled in me the value of a good book.

Thank you to my family and friends who were so supportive during this process. Their excitement, mixed with my own, was such motivation. Thank you to my best friend, Elysse, who is awesome and deserves thanking. From the beginning, your level-headed advice has helped steer me in the right direction.

To my brother, David, your passion for music is my reminder to do what I love. You may be younger but you still inspire me.

But most importantly, thank you to my beautiful Mom. I have always received your support and having it has meant everything. With each new opportunity that comes my way, you not only offer your advice but your time and energy. All my life you have been a model of selflessness, giving more to others than to yourself. I love you for that and appreciate it deeply. Thank you for always being there.

About the Author

Lauren Elise Donaldson is a photographer, stylist, and design blogger behind LaurenEliseCrafted.com and *Cottage Journal*. As a child, her creativity and craftiness were always fostered, which eventually led her to design school and to a degree in architecture from the University of Southern California. After residing in Italy, impassioned by the beauty and culture found there, she refocused her energies on supporting the handmade and independent craft movement. Fostering that lifestyle, she uses her lens to capture her own stories of craft and simple, creative living. No matter the project, her goal is to inspire others through the act of making.